THE
DELIVERANCE
OF
MARLOWE BILLINGS

CADIZ MUSIC
2 Greenwich Quay, Clarence road
London, SE8 3EY
www.cadizmusic.co.uk
Email: info@cadizmusic.co.uk

Cover and Book design by Javier Rosas Herrera
www.javierrosasherrera.com

Copyright © 2014 by Dan Stuart
www.marlowebillings.com

Published in 2014 by Cadiz Music Ltd

All rights reserved. No part of this book may be reproduced in any form or by any electronic or mechanical means including information storage and retrieval systems, without permission in writing from the author. The only exception is by a reviewer, who may quote short excerpts in a review.

This book is a work of fiction. Names, characters, places, and incidents either are products of the author's imagination or are used fictitiously. Any resemblance to actual persons, living or dead, events, or locales is entirely coincidental.

Printed in Oaxaca, Mexico

First Printing: February 2014

ISBN: 978-0-9571717-2-5

I ALWAYS LISTEN TO WHAT I CAN LEAVE OUT

— MILES DAVIS

THE DELIVERANCE OF MARLOWE BILLINGS

A false memoir by Dan Stuart

OPENING

OKAY, IF WE'RE GOING TO GO ON THE ROAD TOGETHER WE BETTER GET A FEW THINGS STRAIGHT. FIRST OFF, EVEN THOUGH THIS BOOK IS ABOUT MY DAYS IN THE MUSIC JIZZ, I'M NOT FAMOUS.

A tad infamous maybe but not widely known at all. That doesn't mean I didn't *do* anything, it's just what I did (and people like me did) was secret, invisible, charmed. I've also changed most of the names so even if I'm talking about someone or a company you've heard of, you'll still have to do your own informed guesswork. Second, I'm not a particularly nice person and if I have to worry about whether you like me or not then we're both wasting our time. Finally, there is no real plot because I refuse to impose a false arc on these events in order to make it all digestible to middlebrow sludge. If you're fine with all that then read on friend, read on. If not, put the book down and pick up some other post-punk tale of sin and redemption.

You'll find none of that here, I promise.

Dan Stuart
OAXACA, MEXICO / OCTOBER 2010

THE DUDENS

WE WERE THE *DUDENS* BEFORE *THE SERFERS*. Me and Grum against the world.

Until it became *The Marlowe Billings Rock Show*...

"Fuck LA, can't do it, I'm going home."

Grum's Datsun B-210 is idling at the curb, he got a jump from some sympathetic Mexicans and doesn't want to ask again. I'm drinking a beer in the shower and Grum's words echo in and out of the fog. I want to talk him out of it but...

"Hey I rolled a couple for the road and grabbed that twenty on the table, sorry man..."

I wasn't too concerned. Shit, Big Dog had just moved in and seemed mildly interested in the band. Who was Grum anyway but my best fucking friend?

Robin was more upset than me. She loved Grum and anybody else that threw a chin out. She was our cheerleader, a den mother deluxe for the depraved and desperate.

Woman is the nigger of the world...

I first heard Patti Smith at another Duden's house, Jesse. *Good* guitar player. His father was a lawyer gone bad when that still meant something. Rags to riches during puberty, couldn't have been fun. Jesse had a genius older brother who pissed on people's steaks to put himself through college. That was a missing link, the angry hippy and the disgusted punk. Peace and love?

Sure, *go for it.*

We Dudens were everybody's little brothers, all middle children. Parents divorced or should be. Out of weed, we raided daddy's stash and laughed when he couldn't figure it out. Our mothers were unhappy and more confused than us. They had affairs or went on Est seminars and came back with nasty grins of determination. It was an ugly time to be an adult but great to be a kid, free and alive and completely fucked up.

The problem came later when we had to follow it up with something.

Grum was a throwback, something lurking in the woodpile. Grum's dad was a gynecologist to the stars but *his* daddy was a saw playing blind man from Arkansas. Grum always felt that tug but never gave in. If he had, he might not be serving 20 months in a federal pen, shit he might be writing these words instead of me.

Maybe he still will, put me to shame.

We loved each other, me, Grum, Jackson and Chez.

Brothers... *Dudens.*

We wanted to love Big Dog too but he wouldn't let us. He wasn't a Duden or a Serfer, just a sweet Irish Mexican with an erratic kick drum. But fuck it, we weren't playing disco, only cleaning house to that relentless beat.

Born, born, born... born to be alive.

Fortunately, Billy accepted our love and his imagination carried us all the way to Memphis. Little brother, nobody's fool. Lost his virginity the first time in a mental hospital, and the second time in D.C. when I broke my fucking toe playing barefoot. Too drunk to play, they threw us out with a *never come back.*

Damn, a good gig too with cute bartenders and clean toilets...

Billy go back in there and get our money...

So yeah, the Dudens grew up in a desert, beautiful but uninhabitable in the long run.

Let me try to explain my generation in a way like Fitzgerald did...

I'm serious.

A FEW NOTES

SONGWRITING IS EASY.

Don't pick up that shitty old guitar until you have to. Be fucked up but with the clarity of a monk. Fear noodling and embrace the obvious. Keep the windows open, it's just notes and shit.

I always wrote songs, a lot of people do. It's no big deal. The performance of something counts more, sorry. The Bard kicked ass because the punters wanted to roll around in his mess, get covered in it.

Actors want to be musicians and musicians want to be painters. Writers are fucked, but happily so. Whoever is your patron determines your muse.

The audience is an illusion.

I am the audience, you are my slave.

Eat me raw, balls and all, don't stop there, have some hair.

I heard that from a ten year old philosopher back in 1970. He was picking his nose and flicking boogers at the girls.

It still makes sense.

I was and still am a lazy writer. They paid me to be lazy, to be stupid, to stay fucked up forever.

He tried to do his best but he could not…

Who can?

WHAT WERE WE THINKING?

I LEFT HOME ON FATHER'S DAY... a terrible kid, self-righteous in the extreme.

Sulking, I accuse my neurophysiologist Dad of being part of the *military industrial complex* when all he's really guilty of is taking me to good foreign movies and killing a cat or two for science. In response, he squishes my face like a melon while dear old Mum flushes my buttweed down the toilet. Wanting the final say, I piss around the house like a spoiled poodle for the next couple of months. I especially enjoy peeing on their bed.

I should have been put *down*.

So I left the womb and rented a house with Grum, the soon to be legendary *Serfer Hollow*. Grum and I went way back as little kids, swim team and football, and later smoking weed before first period biology. He was a sweet guy with a fearsome look that attracted trouble always. Fortunately, he had a wicked right hand that would come out of nowhere to devastating effect. I personally saw him knock out three or four cholos, a brother or two, not to mention the odd redneck.

Not all at once, but still.

Rich kids, we voluntarily bused ourselves to Tucson High in a program to enhance the ethnic balance. That made us *white boys* and targets for a little score evening which did us both a world of good.

I suppose.

It was Grum who first turned me on to glam: Bowie and the Dolls etc. He assured me that cocksucking wasn't a requirement. He also played the drums which was the first thing he brought down to Serfer Hollow from his parents foothills mansion.

We were halfway there.

I still dream about that summer. I was a lifeguard at a barrio pool where I'd arrive every morning on my little Yamaha. Friday nights, I'd work the door at Pearl's Hurricane downtown where a punk scene was emerging.

One night I let this cute chick in… Robin.

She was back from LA for the summer where she'd been attending design school. LA, yeah. She had big hair and a big ass and the sweetest disposition on the planet. She had gone out with Odie for awhile who was the first person I knew to die of AIDS.

But that was later, much.

That summer of 79 wasn't 1969. Sid was no Manson and the eighties would be our party where we made the rules motherfuckers.

Create what you want, don't sell out.

Ice cream for breakfast?

Go ahead, lap it up before it melts.

PICKING AND GRINNING

I WANTED A BANJO.

I really liked Roy Clarke. He showed up on all sorts of shows like Mike Douglas, Johnny Carson, Dinah… must have had a great agent. I wasn't into Hee Haw yet, that would come later when a cool cousin from San Francisco gave the thumbs up. Even still, Buck Owens took awhile, too much corn. Now I can't get enough. What a genius, everything tuned down a half step, a tad dark.

The woodpile.

So I wanted a banjo but what I got that Christmas was a cheap Mexican guitar. A *classical* guitar no less and lessons with an old rummy at *Beaver's Band Box*.

Sounds like a porn movie, I know.

After the first couple of lessons, the foul breathed drunk gives up on teaching me to read and just shows me some songs.

That old gray mare ain't what she used to be…

Well no shit.

Holding down those strings was brutal at first, sheer agony. Any sensible person would just give a kid a little folk guitar in open tuning and let him make some noise. But those were the days of the Suzuki method and other happy horseshit. Blues was *nigger music*, like giving a third grader heroin or something.

But I learned those cowboy chords, yes indeed. I couldn't read a chart to save my life but I had enough of a vocabulary to write a tune or two and damn if I didn't start. The only problem was the better guitar players I knew wouldn't play lead to any of the chord progressions I came up with... something furtive about it that they just would not accept.

Dangerous even.

I got a decent little Yamaha a little later. Hundred bucks. I liked that guitar so much I later bought one of their motorcycles.

As for banjos, I pretty much hate 'em now, unless it's Ralph Stanley or someone...

Americana, *what a ghetto.*

SID & NESTOR

SERFER HOLLOW.

A masonry stucco gem with a car dealership to the rear and the Green Dolphin next door. The car lot we pilfer for batteries and such and the bar we never enter except to play an occasional game of Space Invaders. Bored, we like to shoot bottle rockets over patrons' heads as they stumble out. Not amused, two cowboys come over looking to kick butt just as the nasty yet charming Nestor drops by with his pit bull Sid.

Nestor and Sid were later participants in the *great punk rock parrot murder of 1979*.

I offer a lit joint to the rednecks but Nestor has Sid snapping at their balls. Yelling at Nestor to take Sid inside, I turn around to apologize when the meaner of the two pushes a rifle barrel into the center of my forehead.

"This is Tucson Arizona you little faggot, I should shoot you right now."

"Do it then... do it, do it, do it!"

He slowly lowers the barrel.

"You crazy fucking punk."

I puke up a Circle K bean and cheese burrito as sidekick drags his friend away.

Shit, that was *dinner*.

Back inside, Sid gives me an evil little grin.

I hated that dog and every pit bull since.

Death and angels on the ground, death and angels flying around…

THE ONE, FOUR & FIVE

THE FIRST SONG I WROTE WAS "APACHE PRINCESS". It sounds dumb but I had gone to an Indian puberty rights celebration a few weeks before. A friend of my Dad invited the family. He was a Bronx Jew who had married into Mescalero Apache royalty after meeting his bride at Yankee Stadium.

The Indians won, 3-2.

I'm barely thirteen years old and already smoking weed and the whole thing is very trippy with guests drinking some sort of tea that I doubt now was peyote but they all claimed it was. The initiate was this chunky beauty who looks totally embarrassed about it all on one level but on another quite proud. She puts a smudge of corn pollen on my forehead, says a prayer and voila I'm fertile.

Need some now...

One weird thing was the fry bread had a metallic taste, similar to the feeling of a cold spoon against the back of one's throat after shooting morphine.

I'm sure you relate.

Years later after raiding a doctor's black bag in Scandinavia, I would remember that taste and dream of the Apache princess who had become a woman before my eyes.

I've been looking for a lover but I haven't met her yet…

So that was my first tune. Open chords, most likely in E minor and more importantly words written on paper to be sung. I played it for my little sister and she kinda freaked out. How could I do that? Was it legal? Aren't you supposed to learn other people's songs first?

I skipped all that, wasn't a good enough player anyway.

But I knew I could do it.

THAT'S A *GOOD* GUITAR

SERFER HOLLOW BECAME a collection pond.

Jackson made three, a cool little dude with a bitchin MG. He was friends with our older brothers, the guys we bought weed from. He liked to talk music and started coming around the Hollow on a regular basis. He was from Queens and it showed in ways we really couldn't put a finger on. To us, everything east of the Mississippi was Europe. He had a street savvy that we lacked, a certain toughness mixed with a quixotic nature. Years later we should have listened more to Jackson and his up from the gutter worldview that Billy always made fun of. Jackson knew how to work for things whereas Grum and I preferred to just get by.

Punks... Dudens.

One day Jack took me down to the Chicago Store and told the owner Lou that we both had jobs and we needed a guitar and bass *immediately*. I picked out a candy apple red Mosrite and Jackson fondled a heavy SG. We signed the loan papers and flew back to Serfer Hollow to show Grum.

"Well heckus... check it out."

"Don't touch... that's *my* guitar."

"C'mon ya dick, let me see it."

"I'm serious, don't touch it."

"You're such an asshole Marlowe..."

"We need some amps... a microphone."

"Shit yeah... Jackson?"

"I'm working on it... I already got us a gig."

"Jesus Christ!"

"Don't worry, I know a little PA we can borrow... no one's gonna care what we sound..."

"Fuck I care dude, Marlowe?"

"I got some tunes... how hard can it be?"

That eternal question.

BLOW ME MAURY

NO ONE PLAYED VERY LONG. 10 songs, maybe less.

If you played too long no one trusted you. What next, a guitar solo?

Better not sound too good either.

People forget it could be anything and still be punk. *Anything*, didn't need a guitar at all.

Saxophones came back in spades... *Oh bondage, up yours!*

The most punk rock thing I ever saw was The Killer playing a country music festival in Scandinavia. The vein on his forehead was just *throbbing*. We had this black Amazonian soul singer in the band and he so disturbed her she couldn't sleep for a week. I liked Victoria but Billy thought she was a Victor. I would have let her suck my dick either way, better than the family Hoover I'm sure.

Punk means never having to say you're sorry...

ROCK FUCKING LOBSTER

WE LANDED CHEZ courtesy of a clever blonde.

I get a reltney just thinking about her large yet perky tits. Carol and I were always at odds, when she came to visit us in LA I stuck a steak knife in a dolls head and impaled it through her pillow.

Voodoo shish-kabob.

Carol really deserved better even though she was fucking with Chez's head and freeloading to boot. Gorgeous tits get you only so far, even in LA.

She did do us a favor once, more than a favor…

She made us.

Chez was a very talented cat but with an odd sense of taste. He worshipped the Residents and not in a fuzzy conceptual way. Just superwhite all around, loved puns and cowboy boots. I always felt like hitting him. He was one of those people that despite his impish charm you just knew was capable of murder. Under the jokes and giggles he seethed and twitched and that's how he played the keys.

He really defined our sound until the kid showed up.

In Tucson, Chez had been playing with this punk/new wave cover band. They were all pretty good and it pains me to think *they just didn't get it*. It shows how horrible some hometowns can be, where you have to play someone else's song to please a crowd that ain't going anywhere anyhow.

Debilitating.

The drummer in Chez's first band was a rich junky from the foothills who went to prison for robbing a Dairy Queen. He was one soulful motherfucker and loved music more than anyone I've ever known. His passion was contagious and he resented me deeply when Chez joined the Serfers.

Sorry Duden.

Now remember, Chez just wanted to get into that blonde's pants and when she told him to tell us he was interested in joining the band, he listened. She was deep and devious and could *hear* what was needed...

Thank you Carol...

Since we only rehearsed to learn new songs, we told Chez to just show up at our next gig and bring that funny Fender organ. He knew the songs well enough to vamp along and a din emerged... a frothy cocktail of some Doors and Sir Douglas, with a splash of Talking Heads. Okay okay, that sounds better than it was but there was something happening worth pursuing and maybe even more mysterious than Carol's sweet pussy.

So that first show with Chez was a huge success. Afterward, the entire audience of maybe 20 people retired to Serfer Hollow for drinks and mayhem. We told Chez that if he needed a place to stay, there was a bed in the basement. Happily he went down to take a look but popped right back up.

"Dude are you okay?"

Hands shaking he looked crazed. He downed a beer in one swallow.

Que pasa?

Down in the bowels of Serfer Hollow, Chez had stumbled upon the object of his desire sucking Jackson's not insignificant cock.

Jackson later claimed he *didn't do nothing to no damn body...*

Lesson #1: never admit to getting your dick wet.

Welcome to the band!

JUST CRIMINAL

THE JUSTIFICATION WAS ART, permission granted.

I was never much of a thief but appreciated crime in a French sort of way. I needed something loud and I knew how to get it...

The Pete Townsend method.

Slinking across Broadway, it's easy enough with a brick through the window and a quick grab of a thankfully light solid state amp. The alarm is deafening but the streets are empty and I only have to huff about a football field in length back to Serfer Hollow. The problem is the faster I run the longer it takes, like I'm traveling against the rotation of the earth. Head spinning, I finally make it back to the laughter of all who've been watching from the porch.

"A Crate? You stole a fucking *Crate*?"

"Plug it in, let's hear how it sounds."

"What if the cops hear and put two and two together?"

"Look the cord's missing... sliced it off pulling it through the window."

"Shhh, listen. The alarm quit ringing, turn off the fucking lights."

"Stash that piece of shit somewhere... a Crate, you committed a felony for a Crate!"

"Fucking Marlowe, too fucking much dude."

The next day I went and found a cord and spliced it together. The amp sounded horrible but I was happy. It's like a first car, who cares? We had a gig that Friday and I was worried that the cops would send a detective out checking to see if anyone was playing a shitty Crate. Hilarious now thinking about it but it was real enough at the time. Breaking the law like the leather queen sang and don't forget The Clash had already covered Bobby Fuller covering the Crickets.

Heady stuff if you buy into it all.

Months later, when the cops came around for real after a less righteous smash and grab I would have second thoughts. Till then, I was happy that my candy apple red Mosrite finally had a girlfriend to plug into.

Yesterday was the day I saw her...

VETERANS OF FOREIGN WARS

THERE WERE MAYBE THIRTY PLACES TO PLAY… *in the entire country.*

Word got out fast that Tucson had a gig and soon they all showed up. We would usually open due to favoritism with the local promoters who also owned the neighborhood record shop. Unsung heroes.

Weeks before, I dreamed about the weird poet chick with the righteous boyfriend and the rockabilly guitarist who was always smiling. They were most impressed when we showed up at the club hauling our shit in shopping carts. At the after hours party my dream was realized in startling detail like a play read but not seen. The grin disappeared as rockabilly sighed:

"Don't you have any cute chicks in Tucson? They all look like drowned rats."

For a lot of punks, crossing the Mojave was a shock. The Ford Econoline is the work horse of musicians everywhere but keeping the AC functioning is seldom a priority. There was a fantastic band from Vancouver that came chugging into town with their Eskimo drummer close to death. Someone took pity on him and brought him to their parent's house where he could sit in a pool all day like a polar bear at the zoo. Heat stroke struck again at the gig. A cute bartender soaked a towel in ice water and wrapped it around his head like a turban. Like so many great bands back then, the members reassembled into other groups or just went off to college with a shrug. No one knew you could do both, that came later.

Much.

Of course there was a fight every night. The main trouble was the burnt out vets and crazed hippies who didn't like their bar being used in such an unpatriotic manner. As a long haired kid, I was used to adult males calling me a girl and now just a few years later they didn't like the short hair either.

"You know what a punk is boy? That's who gets fucked in prison."

"Why you wearing those jungle pants punk? I slogged through Nam in those, take 'em off motherfucker!"

"Fuck you! My Dad died wearing these... he came back in a body bag!"

"No shit, sorry kid... I didn't know..."

"Whatever... you dudes gonna pay the cover or what?"

We had our protectors though. Quiet fuckers who had seen some real shit and liked this punk weirdness. Having a large university nearby helped as well; many made the connection between 69 and 79 and liked the subversion. They'd come down and slum and we'd sneer at the wives thrilling them to the bone. The nights would end at Serfer Hollow and if you lost your purse you could come by the next day to pick it up but don't linger or we'd get nasty.

Like Darby said, *what we do is secret.*

TIRED EYES

KEN'S DEAD, he's in his bed
Black and blue, what to do?
Ken's dead, Ken's dead

The knock came late one Sunday afternoon. The very cute Nancy frantic with Ken locked in their bedroom for hours. We loved Ken, a Baltimore native with stories of John Waters and an awesome backbeat. Best drummer in town, sorry Grum. He also had a monstrous habit and was driving his piss yellow Hornet into pharmacies and stealing narcotics between classes at the U. We had heard the rumors which Nancy confirmed on the run over to their apartment. Why she chose Serfer Hollow as her designated emergency response facility I'll never know.

We break down the bedroom door and there he is, propped in the corner Indian style and cold cold blue. The entire room is covered in pills, vials and syringes as if some degenerate's piñata had exploded.

"Call 911 fucking right now!"

"I promised not…"

"Call 911 right fucking now!"

Lifeguard training kicks right in. Grum and Jackson take turns giving Ken mouth to mouth as I compress his chest and try to count. Chez goes to comfort Nancy but it will be Grum who exploits the situation later. Just like a movie the paramedics burst in and a tough looking little dyke takes charge.

"Up or down? What's the story?"

"Huh?"

"What's he been shooting? Dilaudid?"

"Fuck don't ask me, I just smoke weed."

"Well you're smarter than he is..."

Sure enough she whips out a big old horse needle and stabs it right in Ken's heart. I can't tell you how offended I was years later watching an overrated movie when the bad actress pops up like a jack in the box and the date with Mr. Scientology continues just dandy.

Nothing hip or cute about it, *nothing*.

Ken survived but we all lost some innocence that day. It wasn't just junk, but punk rock that OD'd Ken. He just couldn't reconcile his artistic pretensions with his future security. I ran into him years later at a LA club. He was drinking a gin and tonic and complaining how bored he was with the BMW account of a major advertising firm.

"Shit dude, at least you're alive."

"Yeah I know but fuck, I wish I was doing what you're doing."

Trying to get over?

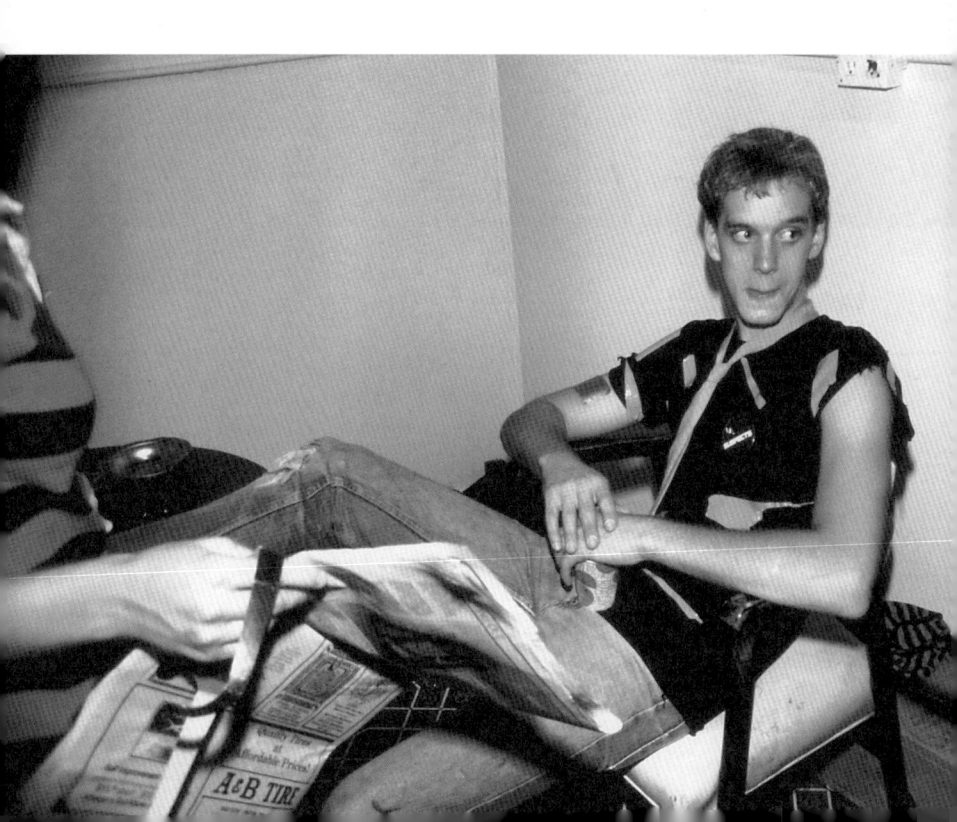

11 A.M.-1 A.M.
MON - SAT

RIOT ON 4TH AVENUE

THEY CALLED HIM DOC.

He ran a club for burnt out hippies and underage coke whores called the Night Train. Punks weren't welcome since we couldn't play and hated guitar solos. Doc got some credit for resisting the disco craze but in reality that would have been cooler. The interior featured murals of magic mushrooms and fairies and he had a *bong shelter* under the stage where he molested drunken teenagers. The cops finally put him away for selling quaaludes, allowing the state to yank his ophthalmology license.

Bummer.

With the punk oriented Record Room right across the street and Tumbleweeds down the block it was no surprise when a riot broke out one night. The fuse lit when a punk chick didn't appreciate some stoner's commentary on her wardrobe. In a flash, fists and bottles were flying and Grum was having a ball landing that sneaky right mongoose of his while Mexican Pete head butted hippies into oblivion.

High on Doc's quaaludes myself, I side-kick some jock with all the force of a butterfly kiss. He knocks me down and starts smashing my head into the pavement while his girlfriend screams encouragement in her torn denim halter. Thankfully, some punk angel breaks a bottle over his head and I roll away laughing hysterically.

Give me some aspirin, give me some pain...

The melee quiets down as several units respond, but the cops are not really interested in breaking up a riot between two of the communities most unpopular subcultures. They sit in their air conditioned cruisers and laugh. The evening ends with an *all are welcome, lick your wounds* party at the Record Room.

"Hey you guys ain't half bad... what's this tune?"

"I like Bowie even if he's a fag... but that Johnny Rotten guy..."

"What are you all so mad about anyway? Just party on..."

"Say what you want, Zep rules, you know they do."

"Fuck Tucson, it's so boring right? So fucking dead."

It's a small world after all...

I-10 NORTH

PHOENIX WAS TOO MUCH TURD in too little water.

We drive up in Nestor's stolen pick-up, all our shit rattling in the back along with half the band. We make the club, full of junky children of the John Birch Society, eyes pinned and hateful. It was so clear how wrong their intentions were, how misguided. They had names like Charlie Monoxide and Marcy Murder and deserved their fates which came none too fast.

I hated the place.

The bass player who wrote "I'm Eighteen" always showed up, that was the best of it.

A few times we played gigs with the two rich Phoenician brothers and that was fine. Their drummer I knew a little from Tucson where we shared a pot dealer. He was in a band called Nuclear Winter. *That* band's guitar player disappeared into the desert after eating too much peyote. The rich brothers took over and it was so similar guitar wise it didn't really matter.

Maybe the guy had split in two after reading too much Castaneda?

We had some mutual friends in LA and played a gig or two at some Mexican bar on Beverly. Now we were back in Phoenix and after the gig I tripped with Robin to shield me from the place. We fucked all night slithering in a sleeping bag across a smooth tile floor and awakened to bad synth music wafting from a back bedroom. In the same skanky black spandex outfit from the night before, our host wondered out in search of her morning wake up shot.

Rise and shine.

A lot of LA punks came from Phoenix. Like the drummer who touchingly named himself after a reporter who had lost all his limbs to gangrene after the mob blew up his car. We shared a courtyard with him and his band for awhile, total vampire junkies who used a coffin for a coffee table.

The paramedics came every payday.

There wasn't much heart in Phoenix. Years later in Paradise Valley, Billy and I ran into a legendary songwriter and producer who had just returned from Sweden after finally paying off the IRS. He had a bunch of Scottsdale housewives lined up doing background vocals that sounded like a locomotive huffing down the tracks.

Now *that's* production.

The legend had stories about everyone, witness the Grievous Angel...

"Oh he'd shoot watermelon seeds if he thought it would get him high."

But the legend was tired of the hustle.

It's hard to keep it up.

SMASH AND GRAB

AN OFF DUTY COP WATCHED THE WHOLE THING.

Grum's dented B-210 pulls up to the curb with me driving. Nestor gets out and wings a brick at the window. Brick trampolines off the glass: *strike one*. Pitch two shatters the window and I snatch the blonde telecaster and twin reverb on display.

Slow motion all over again...

We drive off with a very bad feeling as the alarm fades into the night...

We knew but we didn't *know*.

Back at the Hollow, Nestor senses a perimeter going up and hides somewhere. I roll the heavy twin into the living room with the telecaster balanced on top and close the door. It's a weird feeling, the calm before the bust.

I pick up the guitar and hate the fat neck right off.

Fuck!

The knock comes and I open the door and let them in, no need to wake the judge. The main trouble was convincing them I wasn't Grum and that no, there was only one of us who did the deed. The off duty cop must have been tired and wanted to go home because he let it go. Nestor was splayed flat on the roof the whole time listening for a betrayal that would never come.

My finest hour.

It was a silly caper, I had sold a good guitar for rent money the week before...

Now I was going to jail.

The sun was just coming up as we pass the Chicago Store on the way to county lock-up. The cop did that on purpose, wanting me to see what I'd done. The owner Lou was out front overseeing a big sheet of plywood being put in place. He was still in his bathrobe but didn't look annoyed. I loved old Lou... he had bought out a dozen music stores in the midwest and brought the treasure to Tucson. Musicians came from all over the world to wander through his three stories of everything imaginable. He was a tough Jew who could be found on weekends at the Loft enjoying a foreign movie, his weekly persona dropped for a silk ascot and a cool demeanor.

He had sold me my first real guitar, gave me credit even...

Years later I found myself breaking down in front of the court that had convicted me. I told the story to the bored judge who was about to restore my rights. There would be no expungement however, I still must disclose my felonies but *without any legal consequence...*

Huh? Absurd.

I later tried to live a normal existence but found myself committing felonies in order to hide my record. It was like I was stuffed into a funnel and forced down a chute.

You couldn't get arrested if you tried...

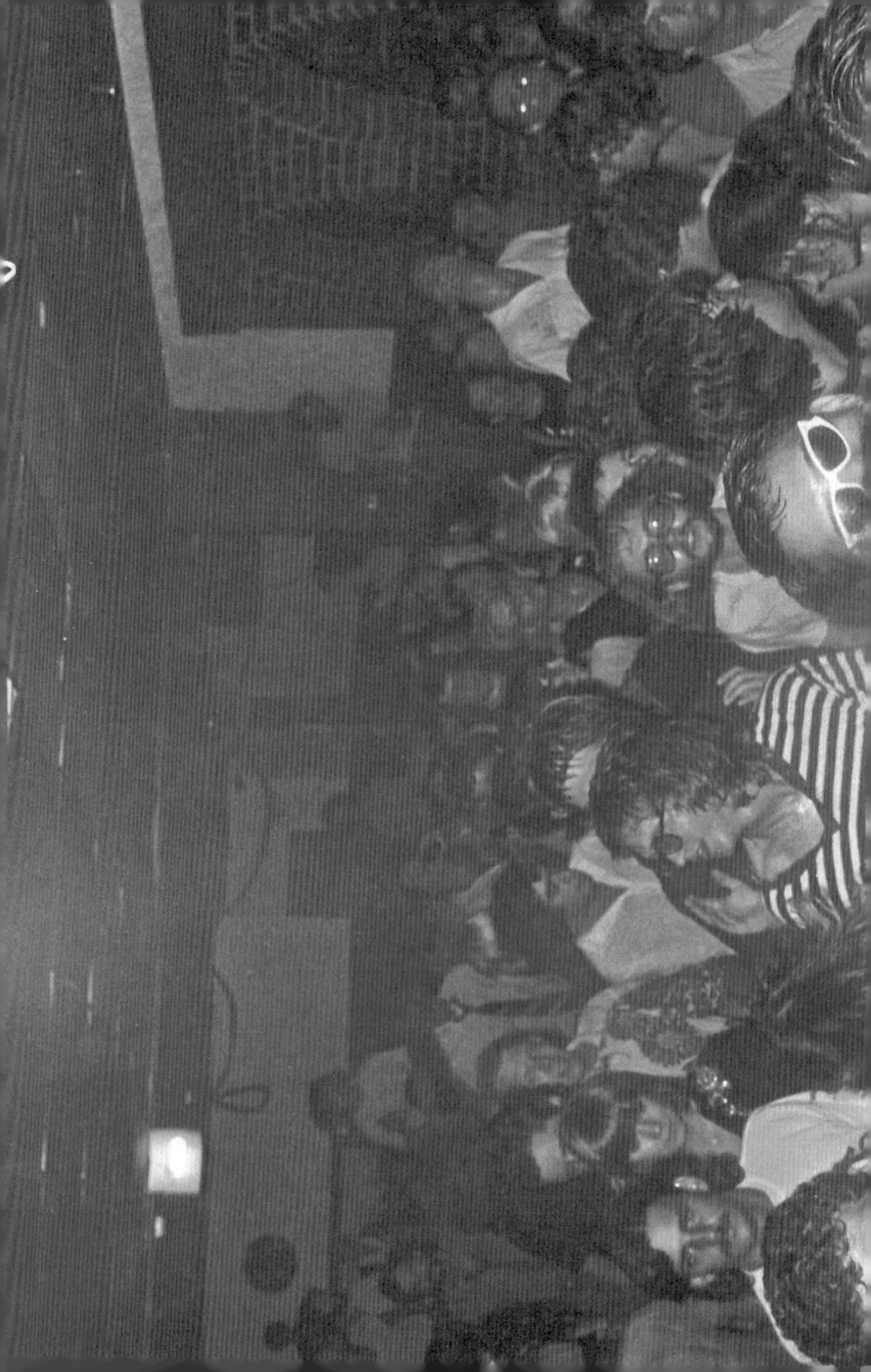

SORRY CHARLIE

IT WAS SO SWEET AND PURE.

We all sounded different and loved one another in ways our boomer hippy parents couldn't even dream of.

It was a small universe, gig and fanzine driven... amateurish in the classic sense. Our first gig was in front of a Factory Legend. He knew Nestor's friends out where a Beatle had a ranch. They arrived in vintage Packards dressed all Clockwork Orange. Still we yawned, that's how much hi voltage attitude there was in Tucson, 1979.

Most of it was good, I assure you.

We were grave robbers, historians sans tenure. Saxophones appeared again magically, honking spit and vile as did cheap organs only a retard could love. It was all on the table, innocent perversity along with a hangdog pursuit of guilty righteousness.

Whatever the moment demanded at whatever the cost.

I know, I know, you've heard it all before but were you lucky in youth? I'll take being eighteen in 1979 any day of the week. Even better, I was eight years old in 69 and internalized it all.

Fuck you Manson, try to get *me* to do your dirty work.

LA WOMAN

THOSE FIRST FEW MONTHS in Hollywood were intense.

I got a job delivering office furniture; that really opened up the guts of the city. I literally ran into Berry Gordy at Motown West and got an eyeful at a porn shoot.

No one ever tipped which I thought strange.

Frank from Philly was the driver and he turned me on to Green's Soul Food right up the street. Frank had been wounded in Vietnam but re-upped anyway when he was assured a cushy gig driving a General around.

Frank moved slow and I learned to follow.

Loading the truck in the morning, these Mae West big boned older blondes would come by the warehouse and whisper in Frank's ear. They all looked like former 50's starlets... he explained he liked a woman with a "fat cunt". I enjoyed Frank, with his Stax cassettes and skinny joints. My lifeguard boss back in Tucson had been a college hoops star and also a brother from Philly. I asked Frank if he knew Herm the Germ? Frank grinned wide, "you mean *Helicopter* Herm."

I couldn't get enough.

Of course my legal troubles back in Arizona made me nervous. Driving along Fountain one day I looked down Las Palmas and saw the police raiding our rental house. Holy fucking shit, what now? I hadn't even been sentenced yet, what was going on? Turns out a Crip boosting crew were the previous tenants and the cops thought they were still there. Gay Paul was the only one home and got quite the rousting. Upon entering his bedroom one of LAPD's finest exclaimed that it "smelled like nigger back here."

Paul had to explain that he also used Jeri-Curls.

I finally had my court date and flew back to Tucson on a one way ticket. I pleaded guilty to the felony but showed proof of gainful employment and prayed that my strategy of becoming California's problem would pay off. Sure enough, I was given probation which was then transferred to LA County under some sort of mutual fuck ups agreement. Reporting to my officer back in LA, he took one look at me and waved me off. He had a room full of Crips and Bloods and here was this little white snot? The guy later allowed me to tour, requiring only that I mail in reports and keep paying restitution. Robin coughed up a grand to replace the window, but I doubt I thanked her.

That was typical.

We finally got our own little studio. I was working down at an electronics warehouse but Robin paid most of the bills. She had a great gig doing the books for a commercial photographer and would eventually rise high in the entertainment world. She worked hard but liked to drink and party so a musician boyfriend made sense. I took every advantage but didn't feel guilty at all. I loved her and that was good enough for me and should have been enough for her, or so I thought. She took care of me and kept me in pot and beer. I returned the favor with slights big and small, refusing even basic niceties. I especially liked to moke on walls after hitting a bong...

Tortured artist.

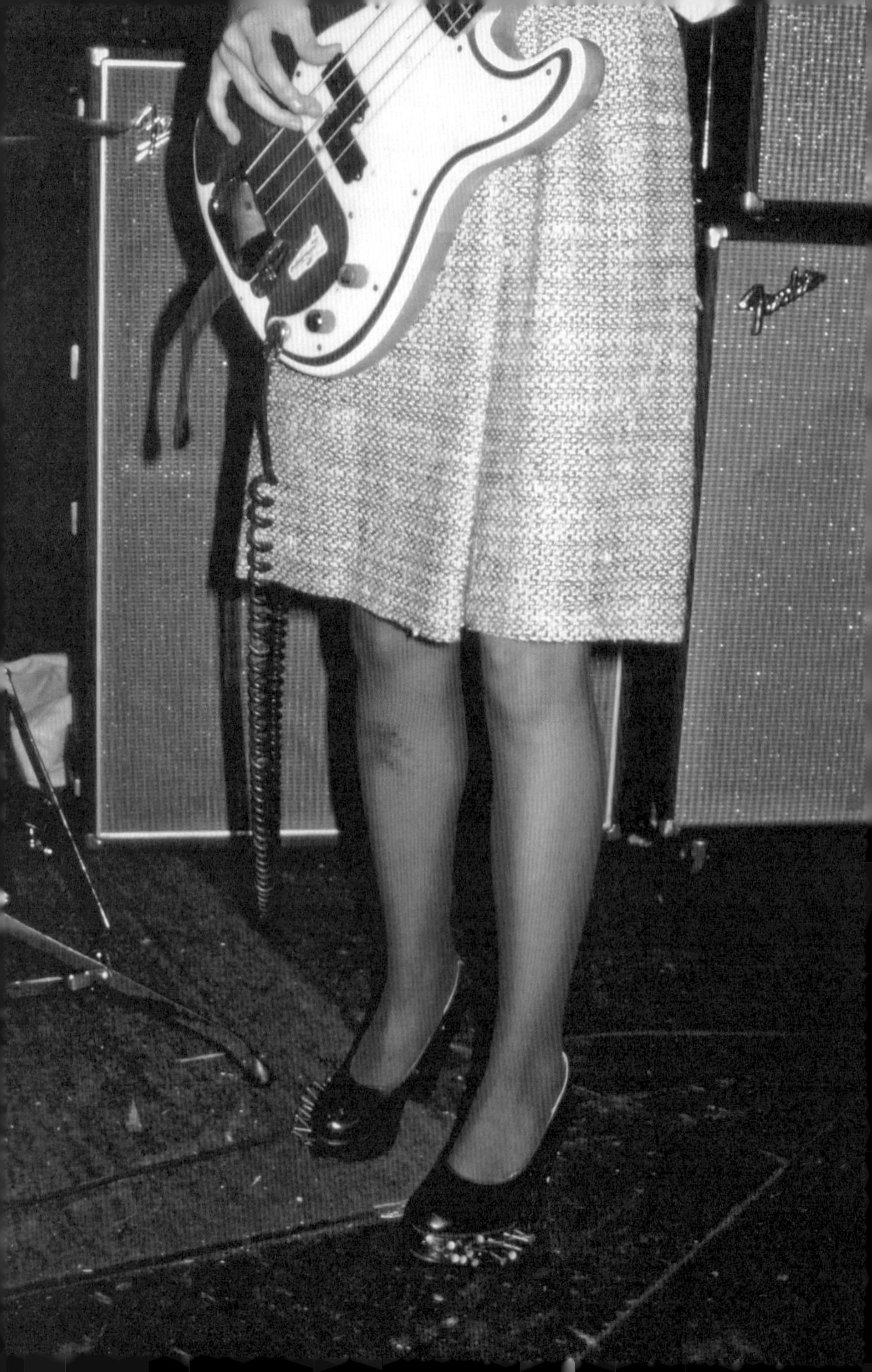
Fender

FREE LOVE

ROCK N ROLL DOES MAKE YOU HORNY, no question about it.

In the Econoline we always had a sleeping bag set up way in the back. One by one, we would take a nap on the way to the next gig and rub one out if needed. I gag thinking about it now, but it couldn't be helped. As far as girls, it often took a couple of passes through a city to get a regular thing going.

All the bands were fucking the same chicks and sleeping on the same floors. These gals would feed and bathe you, share their antibiotics, just generally support the troops. They were also great purveyors of gossip which we all relished. It was really innocent and casual and I would say that people were generally nice to one another.

Truly.

I was on the wrong end of the hospitality stick once living in Hollywood and sharing a house with Robin, Gay Paul and their friend from design school, Milly. This chick was skanky. Strange looking cats would come over late at night and leave her whimpering in the morning, handcuffed to the headboard.

"Someone please, help me."

"Where's the key?"

"He threw it in the toilet."

"Damn!"

"Fish it out with a clothes hanger... hurry!"

The sex stuff was fine, just stay out of the fridge. Not so when Milly told a somewhat notorious punk band that they could hang for a week. The first thing they did was let their half retarded SF road manager spray paint a huge anarchy sign in the street with the brilliantly subtle *Hardcore Rules!* This was the beginning of the end of punk, this new jock/military type of aggressiveness that looked and more importantly sounded stupid.

Not funny stupid... *stupid* stupid.

The worst offender is that pussy who writes really bad poetry and denies he's gay while completely embracing macho posturing of the worst order.

Little Richard could kick all their asses...

KNOCKED UP AND BLOATED

WE HAD A POLICY WHERE WE WOULD PLAY ANYWHERE on any bill as long as there was beer.

It was amazing how few people you could play to and it still mattered. Clubs would open and close but the shows that happened lingered around and festered for months. We opened for Moscow and Hate in the same weekend, complete opposites. The former was down in Slow Death and these rich La Jolla princesses just covered us in spit and not out of affection.

Don't kid yourself, no one liked being spat on and few of us spat back.

After our set, I snuck over to the singer's dressing area and took a big whiff of her panties. Holy moly! She hated us but the boys in her band showed up at our gigs for months, eager to slum. By comparison, Hate and their allegedly notorious followers were pussycats and I always wondered why the singer never became the next Cagney.

By now the old guard was trying to cash in.

Hate was managed by a felonious 60's singer and many LA bands were being booked by the nephew of a famous NY comedian who supposedly had the largest cock in show biz. Not the nephew, an obvious fag who was smart enough to get a certain blonde singer to be his receptionist. It was her that really pulled the strings and established a pecking order of who played where. He remembered me from Tucson where we opened up a couple of times for a really good trio he managed, a band that slipped through the cracks like so many others. It's a cruel hustle.

He told me he would book us *but we had to change our name.*

Seems the famous receptionist didn't like the faux punk bands coming out of Orange County and she didn't want anyone to think we actually surfed or admired Hitler or anything *not really punk*. I had just written a song that sounded like a Rothko painting and I went with that.

It was to be the first of many dubious decisions.

So much of scene making is age based, the young twenties crowd were taking over. We all liked the 60's and wanted to sound like the Animals or the Doors although we would never admit it. Meanwhile, the original punk crowd were approaching thirty and burning out fast. They generally resented us as did the older power poppers who grew up playing Beatle songs...

The punk/new wave divide.

Of course, if you were bad enough to be good and wanted to embrace it all then your music kept changing course like a drunk weaving his way home.

The good shit wasn't done by design, *it just happened.*

After our first "real" record got released I ran into an older punk legend who I really respected. He said he liked it and that it sounded like "Blonde on Blonde"...

I just grinned and sipped my beer.

See, "Blood on the Tracks" and "Desire" were my teenage Dylan records and I had no compulsion at the time to investigate any further with a head full of Borges, Roeg and Pollock fighting for space. I have cohorts who still shake their heads and grimace at my supposed ignorance. The lecture is even in a movie...

Total bullshit.

The library's full when you say it is...

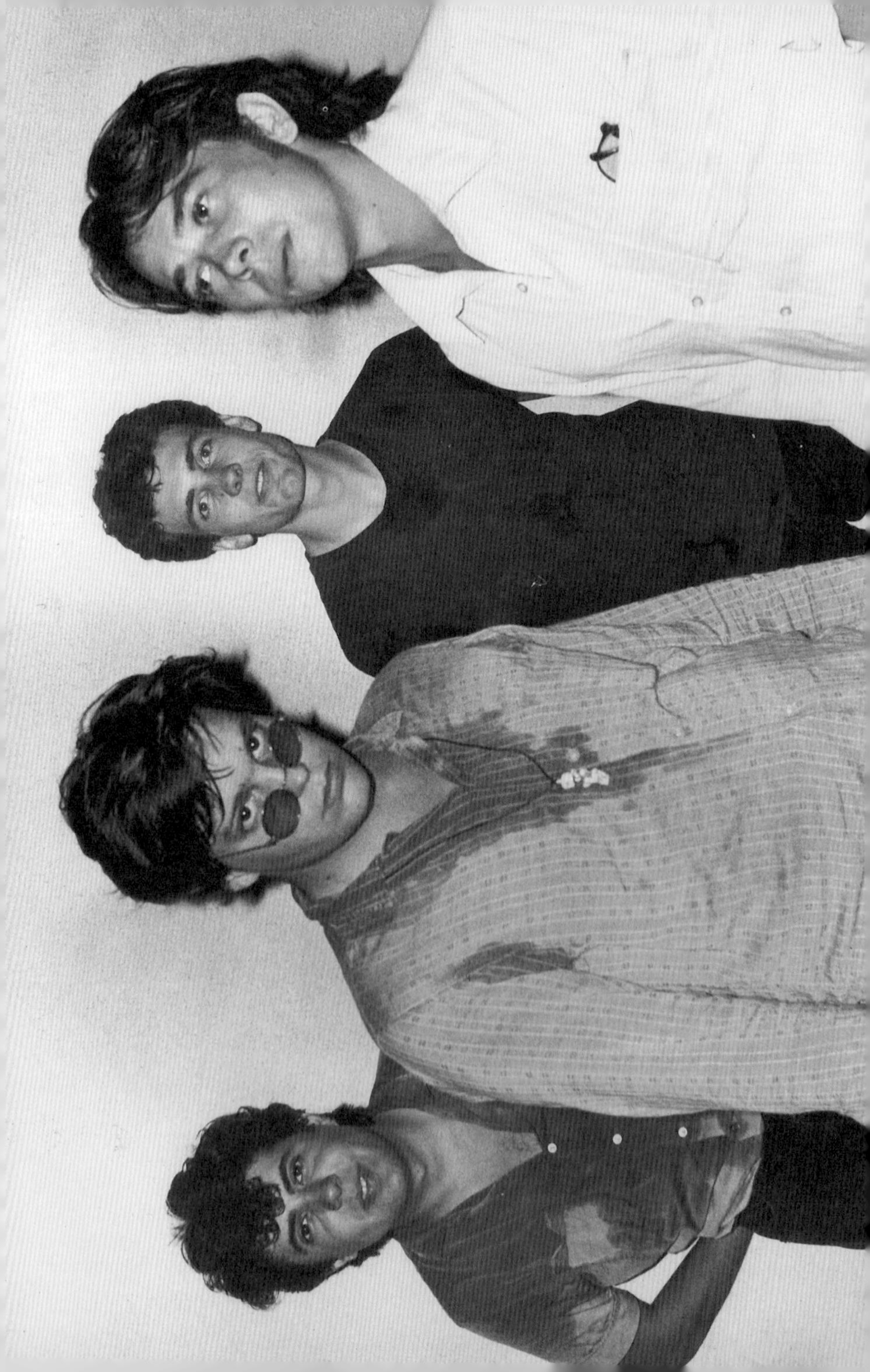

ADAM & LITTLE EVA

AN IRISH MEXICAN SINGER FROM TUCSON said you have your whole life to make that first record and less than a year to make your second.

It sounds good but it's hardly true since there are so many hiccups along the way.

Maybe it was those first couple of songs in the home studio by the zoo? We got lucky, the engineer had recorded The Spiders and The Beans. We finished it up by dinnertime and ran it over to a sympathetic DJ that night. We heard it in AM mono glory driving back to Serfer Hollow.

Goosebumps.

Or was it that moody Englishman's place at Sunset & Vine? A handful of tunes cut with rented equipment courtesy of an adopted trust-funder in the Peace Corp. The Hollywood Ranch Market had just burned down and the boys lived nearby in a crumbly masterpiece with a faded Gloria Swanson at the front desk.

One day they left her a present.

Dear Honey,

Here's a couple of rats and we know it ain't funny, we'll give you two more and call it rent money...

We picked a printer's color sample out of the trash and that was the cover. Pressed five hundred copies on green vinyl and forgot about it. A couple of months later, a letter arrives from Cleveland where a 50 watt station had made it number one. I showed it to Robin who gave me a nice blow job that night.

Better than a Grammy.

Then there was the little eight track where we rehearsed over by Hollywood High. We blew through our set in a day or two and got a nice EP for our efforts. Big Dog was huffing it up and down the stairs since he was doing double duty with a hustling NY poet who was going on the road soon as she kicked. The session engineer was a rockabilly teabag with broken teeth and decent ears. I asked him if the studio had ever been robbed and he pulled out the largest handgun I'd even seen.

"Not lately mate..."

That 12 incher went all over the world. Years later I got a phone call from a notorious widow who loved one of the songs.

"You want to know the *chords*? You mean where I put my fingers? God I wish I knew."

She hung up on me.

Records are like sins...

You gotta go way back to find the first one.

HOLLYWOOD & VINE

DIVE BARS, ROBIN AND I KNEW 'EM ALL.

We loved to go out and drink and compare milieus. The keeps at the Firefly would torch the bar to awaken the comatose, that was amusing. The Frolic Room was a bastion of civility in comparison, but lousy with degenerates. The scene was largely fueled on alcohol with heroin still lurking in the background. Coke was for the New Wave strivers playing their faggy power pop down at Madame Wongs.

I never set foot in the place.

My territorial range in LA was very defined and well marked. This proved fortunate for all the times I would jump out of Robin's convertible, reeling from some innocent remark. It was usually after a show or a night out, I would just hop out at an intersection and walk home. I could usually construe some sort of reasoning for it later, if I cared enough to try. For all my wildness and incoherence I was completely predictable, boring even.

There were some close calls.

Robin had an accountant she had to deal with who was losing an inch or two of intestine every six months. The guy was in chronic pain and rattled when he walked from all his scrips. Robin came home with a gift bag of pills and I settled in for a nice three day weekend. After identifying what I knew, I eyed three or four small yellow candies and popped them down with a Heineken. Ten minutes later I was just conscious enough to tell Robin that I'd made a big mistake and call 911 if I stopped breathing…

Didn't shit for a week.

LA was a great car town if you knew the local streets. Everything was in play except South Central, we generally knew to stay on the white side of Pico. Robin loved discovering thrift stores busting at the gills with the most amazing shit. I think at one point we had about twenty beautiful old radios from the atomic age and before, all in working condition. We ate off of vintage Fiesta dinnerware and spilled wine on our Nudie shirts. Everything was up for grabs, interior design and fashion wise, and everyone had cool shit aplenty. There was no guidebook or uniform, we were free to be ourselves. LA was paradise as long as you stayed outside of it all and didn't get sucked under the shore break. No one saw money yet or cared about the future.

Right now was just too much fun.

That next spring, bands started getting signed. There was this posh son of a CIA officer throwing money around, everyone thought he was English. He came to a show once and said we looked liked bums. Drinking a beer backstage, one of his cute slaves sat on my knee and asked if I was worried about my "career". I was shocked to hear that word, had never used it myself. *Career?* What does *that* have to do with anything?

I still wonder.

MIGHT AS WELL ENJOY IT

TRASH RECORDS WAS A LABEL that had everything going for it except ethics. Don't laugh, punks might be cynical but we believe in fair play.

Trash's image had been created by very talented people running what was first a magazine. A creepy jock sometime porn star poked his head in one day and took it over. No one knew how, maybe an available line of credit?

The jock hired a prissy shirtlifter to cook the books and there you have it.

I still hate them both.

They say you'll sign anything to make your first real record and I guess that's true. In our case, the same lawyers representing Trash were also billing us. The contract itself was a cross-collateralized nightmare that raped us of our publishing. We knew all this but theorized that if we starting getting over then we could renegotiate.

Sure.

That's exactly what happened to the East LA vato legends who got signed along with us. They had a number #1 hit but stayed in bondage for years.

Same old shit.

We got our deal courtesy of a pal heading off with his band to greener pastures. How he managed that isn't clear, but there might have been a nasty call or two from *the trumpet* reminding Trash *who owns the plaza* as they say in Tijuana. In any case, our pal threw Trash a bone by mentioning that they could probably sign this up and coming band with the funny name.

Bingo.

Despite the contractual gang bang, we weren't really bummed out going into the studio. Trash knew we didn't do demos and assigned the house punk to produce. This cat was a stand up guy with his own poetic dreams but would be fired from Trash within the year. Already, older cagey producers in sharkskin suits were coming by the label looking for plunder. There was the Texas bible salesman who charmed everyone and the Cali session guy who had just done the score for an arty porn flick. These fellas smelled money and would go on to hugely successful careers. They had been around long enough to know that the label's trust was key, fuck the artists. Smart yet somehow pathetic. I never worked with guys like them until the end when Billy and I went to the godhead of them all.

Worst record ever.

But not this one, that would have been the end. Ironically, for the first time we *needed* a producer. The house punk kept the vodka flowing and the company away (no easy task) but arranging just wasn't his thing, not that we'd listen. We could have drafted the engineer who came from a great rockabilly and country music family. He was going through a divorce and during breaks would pick up a guitar and play just the most heartbreaking shit. Or maybe there was help next door, Iranian expats playing some of the weirdest pop music I'd ever heard. Instead, we stuck it out ourselves and were left with a half realized gem that was still better than most anything else that year. There were songs and stories about LA and for the first time I allowed myself the luxury of wanging on an open G.

Do you really know what's it all about?

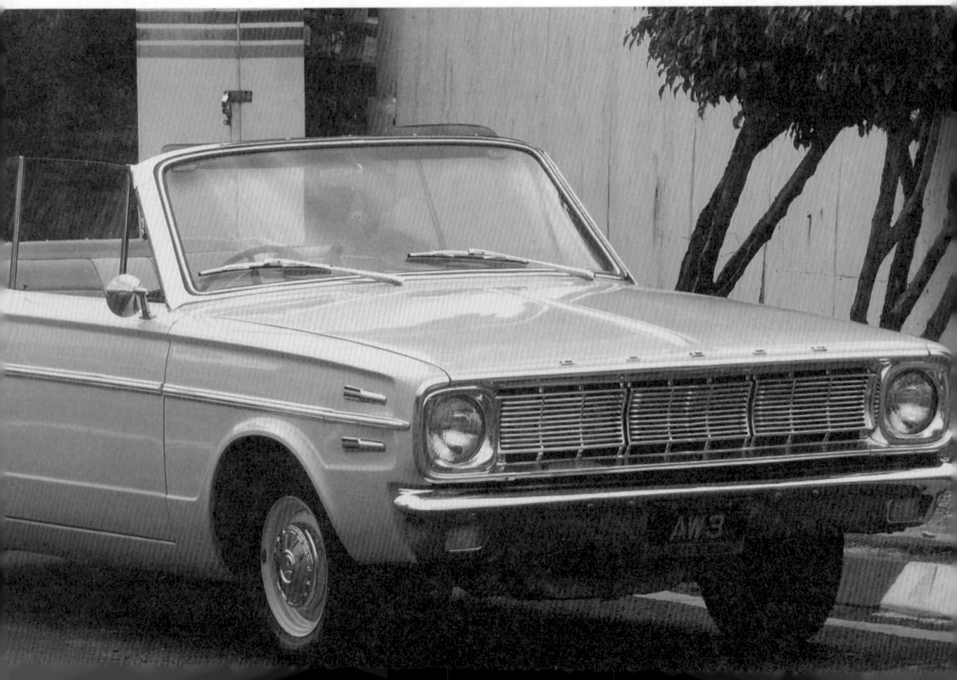
AW-3

LOCUST DAYS

AS A KID, SUNDAYS USED to depress the shit out of me.

In Hollywood though, it was my favorite day of the week. Streets empty, only the Blvd would have any tourists. Even the creepy suburban Dads cruising Santa Monica for fresh chicken would give it a rest. You could get on your bike and ride around and actually breathe. I never felt the weight of the upcoming work week pressing down on me, maybe because I didn't feel trapped by my day job.

I didn't realize until later how bad the economy was in the early 80's.

The number of Mom's living in cars with a kid or two was amazing. You'd see all their shit piled up in the back of a ratty Datsun or Toyota parked in the same general area week after week, usually near some source of water like a drinking fountain. I used to skateboard down Highland to work and I'd catch a glimpse of some haggard Mom with her tweener daughter bent together in some weird pretzel, trying to sleep.

There were bums too of course and the crazies, like the guy who claimed to be related to Geronimo:

I met old Chief down by the store
he told all about his life and more
old dreams die young...

We all had cheap convertibles; you could buy an old slant six for five hundred bucks. One day I was riding shotgun and creeping up to Sunset from a side street. Some whores were hanging on the corner and one walked over, reached down and started fondling my balls. You had to be polite but firm in declining their services or it could get nasty quick. Walking home drunk a couple of nights later, I had to navigate through a gaggle of 'em and realized in the morning they'd lifted my empty wallet. I went back to that corner the next night to get my driver's license but no one would fess up. I even offered a ten buck reward which was the going rate for a blowjob.

One of the funny things about LA is how the city ends at La Cienega and it becomes LA County with the sheriff taking over law enforcement duties from LAPD. Before the 84 Olympics, the mayor authorized a whore cattle drive with mounted officers rounding up the streetwalkers and herding them down Sunset and right into the Pacific... well at least to the county line.

John Wayne would have loved it.

Keep them doggies moving... Rawhide!

GUITAR LAND

AS A KID GROWING UP IN THE 70'S everyone played guitar, everyone.

Wandering around stoned in Indian Ridge you'd hear notes bleeding from every other house. It was blues based jamming mostly, filtered down through the teabag greats and Southern longhairs. No one called it blues, or anything else really. It was riff oriented with soulful phrasing that pleased. Stoner rock for sure and it still sounds great. If you couldn't keep up you picked up a bass or just strummed a cheap acoustic for kicks. No one tried to write anything. Why bother? Kick drum was hard to hear but no one knew how to dance anymore anyway.

Too stoned to boogie.

It was the era of the double solo played in unison in which the two best neighborhood guitaristas faced off and soared. Same thing with all the double drummers, enemy bands would team up and kick ass. With all that weaponry, arrangement skills became necessary and that's where school band practice was put to good use, especially down South.

Of course I'm talking white people here...

The average brother has a different story to tell. White musicians tend to get misty eyed talking about the great soul era but you seldom hear any of the black legends waxing nostalgic. Ripped off and forced to play corny arrangements in their mind.

Slave labor.

As for my own playing, I learned some basic chords but never any scales. Outside of the odd Dylan tune, I didn't have the patience to figure anything out so I just picked out what I wanted. Tuning was always a struggle, no ear. There was a point right before Billy joined where I got a thing going lead wise but soon forgot it in a haze of pot smoke. In actuality, I was very into folk song craft but had no clue that's what I was doing. Those open chord country changes just sounded so simple and right, I thought "Oklahoma Hills" was just the most perfect song. I was searching, trying to get my point across.

That's where Billy came in...

A much too highly regarded English string and spoon bender sniffed later that we were *reactionary*.

He was right.

I wasn't interested in being different anymore, hell we were part of a nice tribe out in LA and were the talk of the town. I wanted to connect the dots and let the ghosts fly. Billy had caught that 70's thing just in time, the last young grommet to receive the wisdom before metal took its course. Never a punk, he was too young to get picked up by the older New Wavers who could have used his skills. Don't laugh, think of the country riffs all over "My Best Friend's Girl".

We were signed to the hippest label in the country and were getting ready to cut another album.

Billy was outside but wanted in...

Hey kid, let's go buy you a good *guitar.*

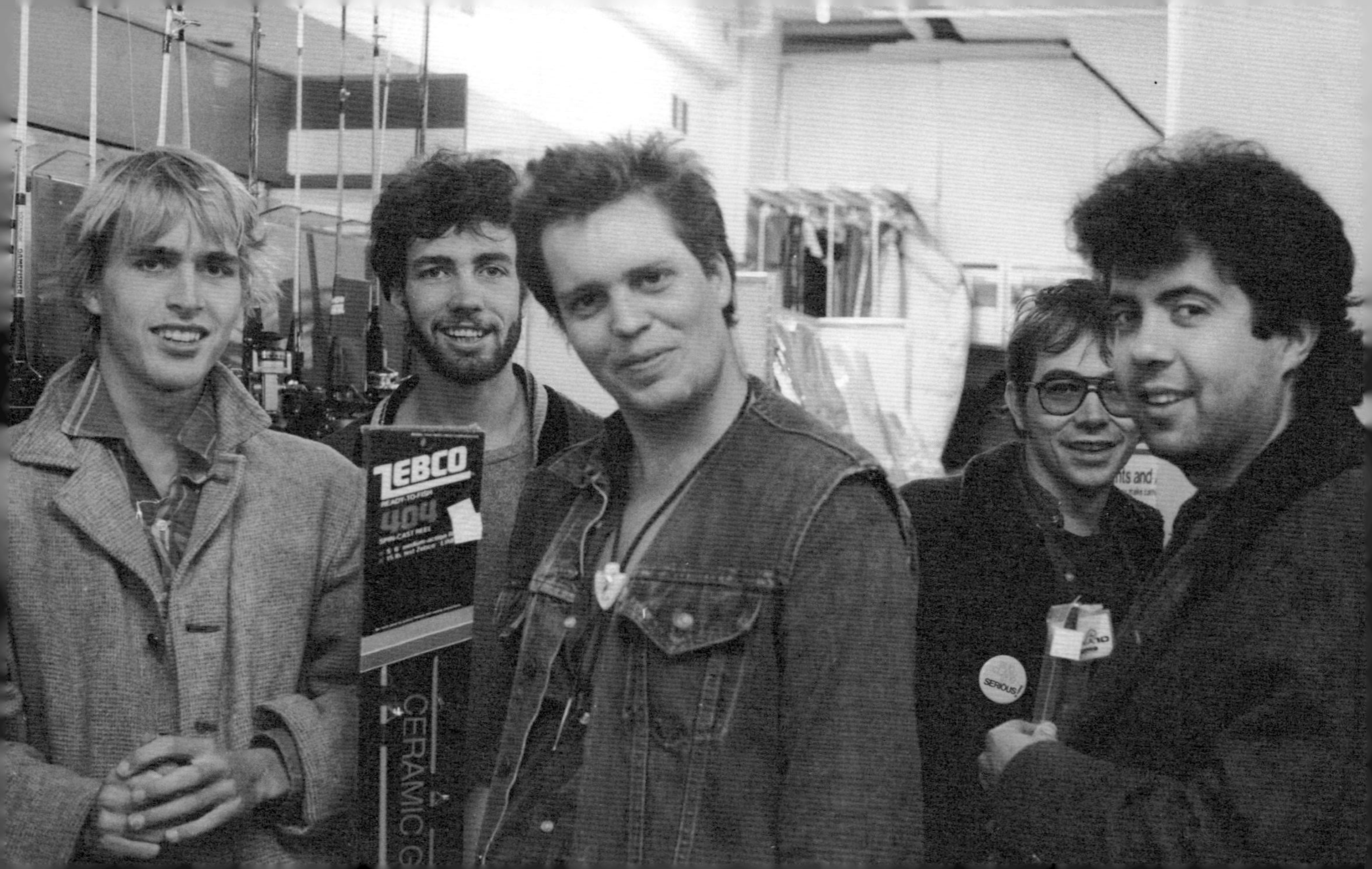
ZEBCO
READY-TO-FISH
404
SERIOUS!
CERAMIC G

BLACK RIVER

FIRST TIME I PLAYED BOSTON TOWN, been driving three days into a strong wind...

The first few hours of a tour are the hardest. Head east from the coast and a malaise sets in, a sickish dread.

Trying to avoid it, we once drove north along the Colorado and found a world of nasty geriatrics huddled down in bomb shelters stocked with Beefeaters, Chef Boyardee and store bought wives.

Best to avoid.

The spirit does lift as the land rises and if Phoenix was not in play we would take the shortcut down to Gila Bend and coast into Tucson. Yeah, fill up on machaca and weed but we seldom played there, just out of spite. It was shocking to drive the empty streets and think that we had just recently been tadpoles in this rain puddle.

Ghost town.

Austin was always a real gig and if you could get past the self-congratulatory nature of the denizens a lot of fun. The problem in Texas are the women: beauty equals stupidity and/or insanity squared. The place was also just crawling with carpetbaggers looking to get laid or famous, hardly mattered which. Shows usually ended badly with my commenting on the locals love of velveeta and ground beef.

Tex-Mex works better as a musical genre than cuisine I assure you.

Oddly, we never played a lot of universities although our first three records all went college radio top ten. That chart meant nothing then, which was fine. The fun was being on the outside with so much sincere support from a few locals in each town who lived for a Wednesday night show. It was like being in the French resistance. The local promoter was usually a sweet college kid and you could sometimes fuck his girlfriend and he wouldn't even mind.

Hey, this is war, some of us ain't coming back.

KEEP ON MOVING

I HATED SKY...

He road managed our first tour and skimmed ten percent off the top. That would make *me* a retard. He had a gravel pit voice, drank gallons of Beam and could snort his weight in cocaine. Little wiry fuck who you wouldn't want to fight. Big Dog knew him from SF, that's how he got the gig. Sky loved Stephen King and read 'em as fast as King wrote 'em. That right there should have got him fired...

A lot of this shit is luck, a good road manager can make a band. Look at piano playing Stu and his *three chord wonders...*

Sky hated TV, especially hospital shows. His girlfriend had overdosed and he forever associated her death with emergency rooms. I met her once and was very impressed, short little brunette with huge tits and a punk scowl. She worked as a dominatrix in a designer dungeon up in the hills. There was a lot of that going on in Hollywood, both Nestor and Riley told me of letting the deputy from Mayberry feel up their biceps for a hundred a pop.

Beats all Andy, just beats all!

Commercial sex was thriving with AIDS yet to do its thing. Big Dog lived in a building up in Los Feliz where working girls would share a smoke while airing out their titties on second floor balconies. He later ran a string of pearls up in SF, a job for which he was imminently qualified.

Made me proud.

Back in the van, outsiders needed to be wary. We pulled a mutiny once in the middle of Scandinavia when some silly baker's son wouldn't give up the wheel. The heat had gone out and we all had on two pairs of pants while stuffed inside plastic garbage bags. We tricked the guy into making a phone call at a rest stop then took off without him. He showed up in Stockholm a couple days later with a mean case of frostbite.

He might have lost a toe.

For all the lack of privacy on tour I've never felt more alone. You withdraw so far into yourself even the Devil shies away. Time, space, distance: it all collides and forms a black hole in the pit of your stomach. Still no matter how alienated, there's a sense of relief that you're not in one of the houses, apartments or offices visible in the yonder. You realize that this was the plan all along, to escape from a certain life of stability and structure.

It's still terrifying.

That you're with your bothers only helps so far...

You can't drive Texas alone.

ARE YOU SURE HANK?

THE CLICHÉS WERE JUST TOO REAL.

Like rolling into Nashville on an empty tank. Clawing between the seats, not enough change to buy a gallon of gas.

We called the promoter who brought us a full can. He was a crazed looking fellow about thirty years old with long red hair and a Stetson. I liked him immediately. We followed him to the club which was a converted diner.
It all looked pretty right.

While we unloaded he played an ancient pinball machine over by the bar.

"Hank Williams fired up this baby."

"No shit?"

"He'd play it for days high on speed."
"Wasn't he born with a tail?"

"Yeah, Spina Bonafides."

"You mean Bifida."

"Well he was a bonafide nut, that's for sure."

He asked if anyone wanted to go to the Country Music Hall of Fame and hands went up. I stayed behind to smoke a joint and take a nap on the scuzzy backstage couch. I awoke to a darkened club and the sound of metallic bangs and clanging bells. I went to take a look.

Hank's pinball machine was all lit up and playing itself.

I wish I was lying.

My hair stood up as the fellas rambled in and hit the lights.
The promoter wandered over and took a look at me and the demonic machine.

"Happens all the time man, you wanna drink?"

He went behind the bar and grabbed several cans of Bud then poured a couple of shots of Beam. Chez got busy sorting through take out containers from the local cafe: catfish, dirty rice and whatnot. Strings got changed, amps checked, the usual shit. The promoter downed his shot and sighed.

"I'm as bad as Hank, crazy for me to drink with my colonic crumbs and all."

"C'mon, pour another one."

"This town turns fuck-ups into us all... why couldn't I've been born in Memphis?"

"I thought you two hated each other... like LA and Frisco?"

"No they hates us but we love Elvis and just want to dance, that's the God's honest truth."

What did that blues harp player say back in Memphis?

I'd rather have a sister in a brothel than a brother in Nashville...

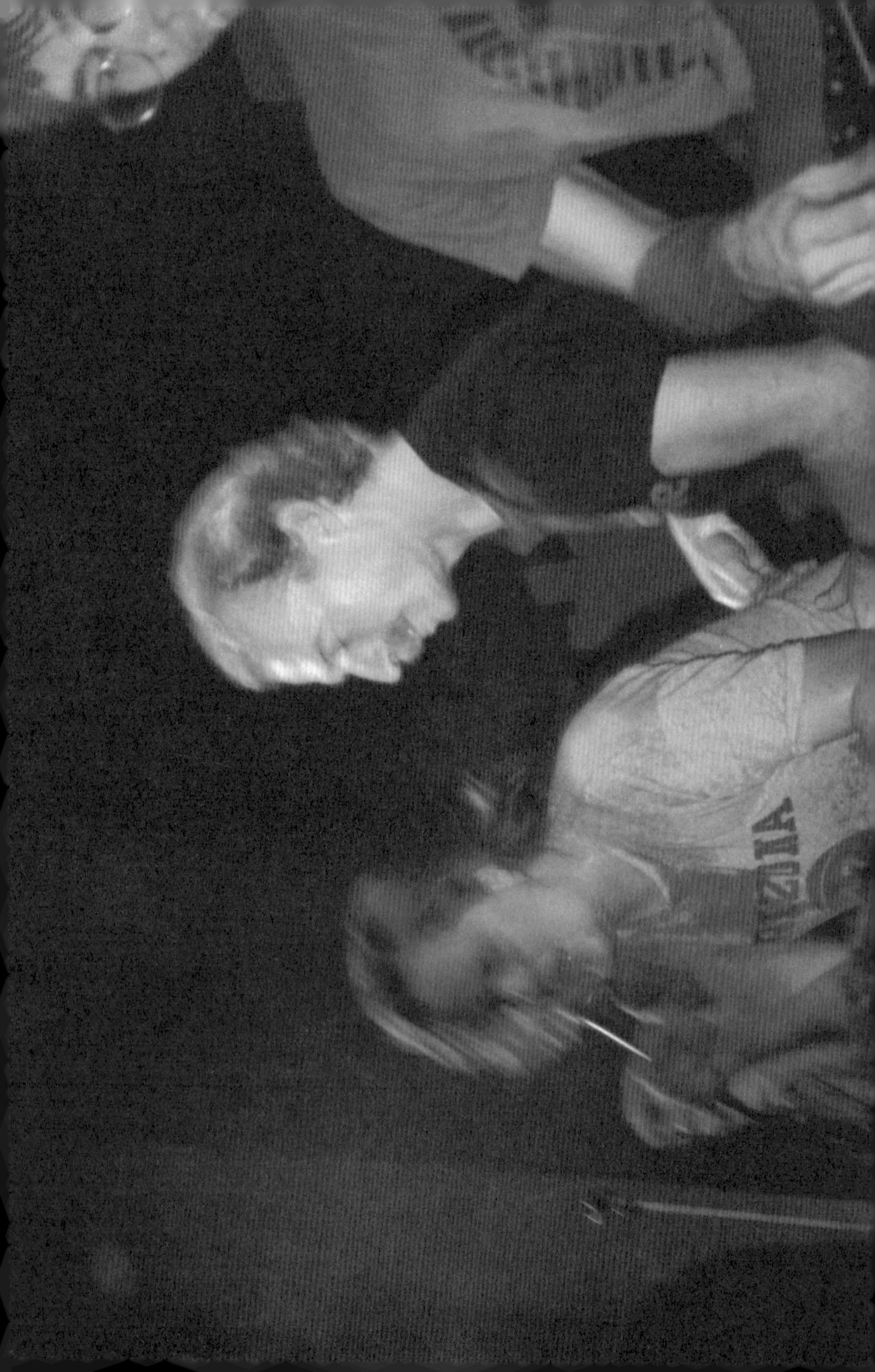

DASHBOARD JESUS

IT WAS RILEY WHO INTRODUCED US TO BARCH.

A good five years older, he was our Stu except he couldn't play. He couldn't tune a guitar either but he was our roadie and that was that. Barch lived in his grandparent's old house down in what is now Koreatown. It was a craft style bungalow with a huge backyard filled up with rusty Model T's and antique farm implements. LA hillbilly shit. A commercial shutterbug took a famous photo of us in that backyard around a fire pit. I found out later he didn't get paid.

No one ever got paid.

Barch was a good driver even when drunk and that was important. We did have an accident once fleeing a hurricane. We were halfway through our set in downtown Providence when the National Guard demanded we evacuate. We loaded up, grabbed our fee and hightailed it inland on eerily deserted interstates. Hauling ass onto a cloverleaf, Barch loss control and smashed into a guard rail leaving us all soaked in beer. The Mutant (Big Dog's replacement) started screaming in pain, his lanky frame snared between two collapsed seats. Everyone told him to shut up which he did after a whimper or two. The soon to arrive state trooper was all business and called for a tow while taking some of us to the closest hotel. He cared less if anyone was drunk, Mother Nature was bearing down and he drove well over a 100 miles an hour.

Scarier than the accident.

Everyone eventually made it to the Holiday Inn where we heard weird creaking and groaning all night. In the morning, I turned on CNN where they were showing extensive wind damage to a building that just happened to be the very hotel we were in.

No fucking way.

The best thing about Barch were the mix tapes he put together, that really helped the miles fly. He took pride in educating us on the holy trinity of folk, blues and country. We had just played Tipitinas for the first time and were heading to Jackson Miss when the AC went out in the Econoline. It was unbearably hot and humid as Barch's beloved Muddy started moaning some timeless lament. That was the first time I really *felt* the blues...

Old black river with the yellow line...

CAMP FIRE GIRLS

NO ONE TOLD BILLY to bring a sleeping bag.

We had a day off and Loon Lake appeared on the map. We often sought out the wilderness, pretending we were frontiersmen or hobos. Barch wanted us to stay with his sister but that would have meant civility and I couldn't be bothered. The boys went along, not wanting to piss me off. They knew I didn't do well up here in Totem Pole country, something about the forest green and grey skies brought out a meanness that scared even me.

It was cold and the whisky and wieners comforted only so much. Light rain, no tent. Around midnight, I got into it with Barch about the Pope. Barch was certainly not a devout Catholic but he defended the faith quite admirably. The short eyed priests had yet to make the front pages, all I had was a Borgia or two plus the Nazi gravy train down to Buenos Aires. I just wouldn't leave it alone and he winged a bottle at me that just missed but nailed Jackson in the foot. Billy, shivering, took it all in wondering what he had got himself into.

Worse than our families...

Cursing, I went down to the shore and put a line in. We had bought some cheap fishing shit earlier in a display of symbolic ritual. What the fuck were we doing? What did we want? I don't think any of us really knew, although Big Dog sleeping in the van was certain he didn't want *this*. Chez needed to be loved and appreciated but I could hardly give him that. Jackson? Order, progress, success. Me? A way to transcend the mundane, to splash myself onto canvas or be imprinted on heavy bond, to escape the rational world of money and logic.

Or maybe I just wanted to stay fucked up forever.

We survived the night and when Barch accepted a morning joint I knew he had forgiven me. The roads were slick heading up to Canada and I felt queasy watching the huge logging trucks scream past. There was no good music that flourished up here, it was all middle brow 70's rock that would later be regurgitated for retard nation to drool over. The kids liked us but I couldn't stand their applause.

Maybe heroin would have helped, or a shotgun.

Later that week I read that a great and famous writer had lost his beloved athlete son to one of those logging trucks. We had passed an accident where a van had rolled and I was convinced that was where tragedy had struck. The writer nearly lost his mind in his grief, he knew it was his fault somehow but couldn't explain why.

It seems no one has any faith anymore...

THE SLOW LANE

I WAS ALWAYS MAKING ROBIN MOVE...

We grew to know the city better than most. We had a great place behind Pinks and a lesser pad above Graums. There was the Clinton house and Mt. Washington, but the apartment she really loved was right across from Paramount Studios. The bosses had built the complex for players on contract back in the glory days. The interiors were impeccably done, most likely by the studio's set designers. Across the street was a leather boothed gem of a restaurant, dark and moody if the sun was too bright.

Old Hollywood, not a bad thing at all.

Right up Gower was a rehearsal place run by a stone cold brother with a mean coke habit and an oldie top ten hit to pay for it. He wore a Stetson with a feather and aviators to block out the noise. Take a letter Maria and address it to *the life*. War, or whatever was left of that very great band, was often next door working on some gritty three part harmony. I'd take a break and put my ear to the wall. It was there that Bubba first heard us and I could tell he dug the weirdness. He always said that if you lived in LA long enough you became it.

Sure, but which LA?

There was so much more to love than to despise.

Like eating cocido with the Rampart robbery detail at La Abeja on East Figueroa. I did that every Thursday when we lived halfway up Mt. Washington. Hungover, I would stumble down the hill seeking *la cura* and salvation... the old abuela shredding pork shoulder while her husband hosed down the cement floor in his Wellingtons. The place was popular with fences and junkies as well, maybe that's why the cops loved it, they could see who had just gotten out of jail.

Believe it or not, I spent little time on the freeways. You could take side streets everywhere and avoid the barely moving clichés. For awhile, I couldn't go on the 405 even if I wanted to since my Dart GT's push button transmission wouldn't shift out of third. I spent my days cruising around under 30 mph and couldn't have been happier.

I still think electric golf carts could solve most of the world's problems.

I didn't replace the Dart's transmission until Robin told me she'd had enough. I needed the power and velocity to get as fast and far away from myself as possible.

I-10 goes both ways.

WHAT I SAY?

HOW MUCH TIME AND EFFORT has been wasted trying to explain the sublime, the temporal, the everything?

Don't get me wrong, we're all guilty here but I'm trying to spare you (and myself) the description of that which dare not speak its name. No, not cocksucking but songwriting. Same thing really, both happen in about two minutes but might take years to finish. Hard to get paid with either endeavor due to fierce competition and the nature of the client.

Supplicants all, that's for sure...

Shoot my pretentious ass before it gets away but it's laziness really and lack of resolve *to hold the fort down* that sets a song free. Leave them holes, people fill 'em in anyhow with whatever they want. Peanut butter for all I care.

I had no problems with writers, painters, actors and such but musicians hated me and for good reason. I said shit they couldn't because they didn't know how. Not that we all have something to say, hardly. A bad musician is just that but a poet?

He could be anything, just ask Dylan.

Was Billy more talented than Chez? No, but he embraced the canon, stocked his library from the mundane to the rarified and embraced it all. Chez, poor guy, wanted to know why something was good, a death sentence. It's like cooking, fuck all the sacred recipes. Sly Stone plus Dolly Parton gives you what? A boner?

Which Elvis, skinny or fat?

Tell me white panties are just that and I'll go down on you myself.

No, I couldn't play and I couldn't sing but they threw a half million dollars at me to keep on trying. Why pay the ransom? To hear the lie you were hoping for all along? Here, let me tuck you in and give you a kiss, it will all be different in the morning when I cash that check.

Sin-eaters are from Africa and I'm whiter than Pat Boone on Sunday. *The blues?* Do you really want to know? It's *nigger* music, best thing that ever happened to the planet. What did Bubba say?

World boogie is coming...

AN HONEST MAN

IT'S COWBOY LONGHAIR'S FESTIVAL to save the narwhals or something.

We go on after Mr. White Lightening himself. How he can sing with a coked up frozen face I'll never know. We play okay but Billy unplugs himself a couple of times all nervous.

"Here's to all the farmers who ate their shotguns for breakfast."

I actually said that.

A redneck guitar legend comes by and wants us to back him up. Billy points out that we can't really play, he walks off confused.

Can't really play?

The rest of the day was field study. I observed that Nashville had better drugs and people tend to be happier because they got paid on a regular basis. Soon half of LA would be living in Franklin Tennessee and making bad pop music.

I would have loved to join them.

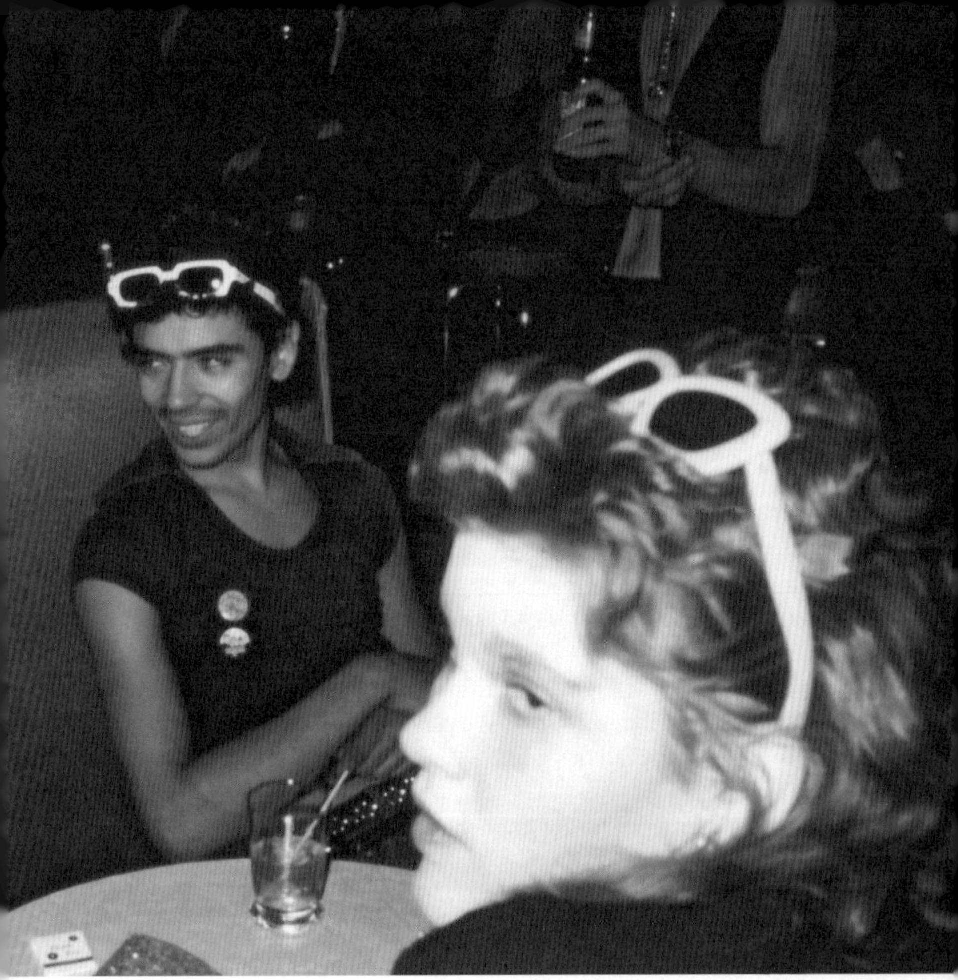

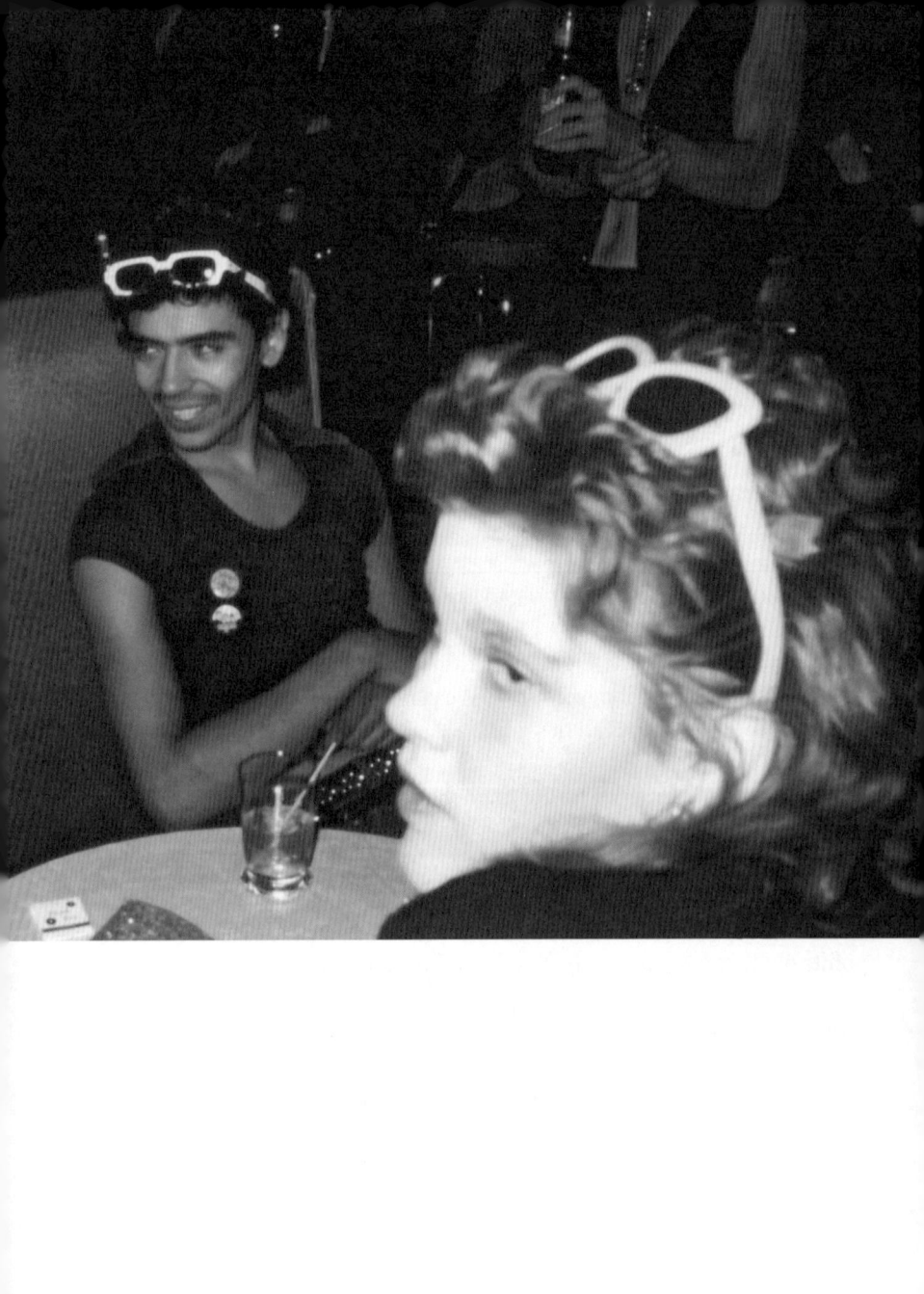

BETRAYED

TWO WEEKS ON THE ROAD when I hear that Robin and Ronnie have invited Nestor to go bowling.

This was always the problem with Nestor, he plowed through people like a killdozer. He was state raised after shooting an older barrio badass who was trying to rip him off, or so he told me. The way he described pulling the trigger was exactly like the knifing in "The Stranger"... that part I believed.

Ronnie by then was unhappily married to a gifted writer who had used a family tragedy to open media doors from coast to coast. The writer must have known that his wife was basically leaving him for his brother whom he had tried to save a decade before. Ronnie herself came from a famous Southwestern family with more skeletons than closets to put 'em in. It was no surprise when Nestor and her went off on a dope fueled multi-state crime spree.

I hated junkies, they gave drug addicts a bad name.

I often lectured Nestor on the topic. Coke was stupid but dope was evil. Strung out in Madrid later, a cloud of darkness seeps under the door and tries to suffocate me. I reach for *Maria* but she's not around, off with saner company.

I still awake most nights fighting for breath, strangled by my past.

Drowning...

Nestor, like most natural criminals, had all the people skills it takes to be successful at whatever struck his fancy. Ronnie was a knock out with a brain but she never got over her love of heroin. It all came crashing down back in Tucson where they had been extorting money from one of Ronnie's aunts who was dying of cancer. The family name kept Ronnie out of prison but the charming Mexican went away once again. Ronnie later claimed she was strung out on Nestor, not dope, but she kept it up for years without him. I saw her once in the 90's with her Mom but couldn't tell who was who. As for Nestor, I wish I still had a cassette he had given me of a couple of songs he had written in LA. Like Manson, it was pretty good and maybe a record deal would have saved some innocents.

I should have sent a copy to Terry Melcher...

I think it was during that infamous bowling night that Nestor told Robin how much I liked black girls. Every punk club would have a black chick or two, especially back East. Unfortunately, I was usually too drunk after a gig to get any proper fucking done, but I sure ate plenty of pussy. Regardless, Robin didn't take that bit of information very well and I'm sure Nestor and Ronnie rubbed it in bigtime. To make amends, I asked our manager Nigel to convince the record company to fly the girlfriends over to Europe to keep us happy and touring. In Amsterdam, they all showed up except my beloved Robin. So there I was, out on the road with all these cunts who were bitching about the deli trays and wondering why it was me doing the interviews.

Worst idea I ever had.

HOLED UP

I FINALLY RECEIVED MY DEATH SENTENCE FROM ROBIN.

It was pronounced soon after getting back from yet another tour. Desperate, I found some vatos to rebuild the Dart's transmission so I could leave town. I planned on Austin but made it only to Tucson where I holed up in Grum's old place, right behind the Boondocks Lounge. It was a little court of bungalows that had been built for the lungers back in pre-penicillin days. I had a tweaker, a comedian and a counterfeiter's daughter for neighbors. A buck fifty a month rent, just like at Serfer Hollow years before.

Too easy.

I spent a lot of time in the Boondocks listening to bad cover bands. Sometimes I'd get recognized and asked if I wanted to sing a song but that was impossible. I wasn't a musician and spoke a different language. Basque? No one could figure out why I was allowed to make records.

Shit, *paid* to make records.

The Boondocks was a sad place and most of the employees eventually got busted for dealing coke. Billy drove down from Frisco once and before his first sip of beer the bartender jumped the bar and knocked a guy clean out. I laughed and finished the guy's shot.

That winter, Robin came home for Christmas and stopped by to make sure. We went out drinking and had a blast but wound up back at my place a little too late. She took in the green wall of moke and tried to quiet the whining black dog that she had saved back in Austin after it got run over by a garbage truck. I swallowed a couple of Vicodins and took a bath, pretending that none of it mattered. Robin came in and sat on the toilet. She lit a cigarette and we watched the faucet fill the tub higher and higher until she finally reached over and turned off the water.

"I love you but I can't live with you. You know that right?"

Misty morning blue is that you by my door?

RING OF FIRE

YOU PLAY ZE ROCK N' ROLL?

So asked the wizard of polka and all things worth celebrating. We were in Nashville recording in his old home studio down the street and figured we should drop by. His new studio was the top floor of an A frame type abode, in the basement he had a ukulele factory going. The wizard mostly hung out in his office drinking Coors and holding court.

First thing he did was to give me a bag of weed.

Goober upstairs was mixing Jesus Christ himself. The wizard would listen in on the intercom and offer an occasional suggestion like *turn the voice of God up.*

This is *it*, how things should be done. The muse is capricious, volatile and forever coy. The wizard knew it was like cupping water in your hand, sip it while you can. When Jesus heard those Mexican trumpets in a dream the wizard believed and obeyed.

He obeyed.

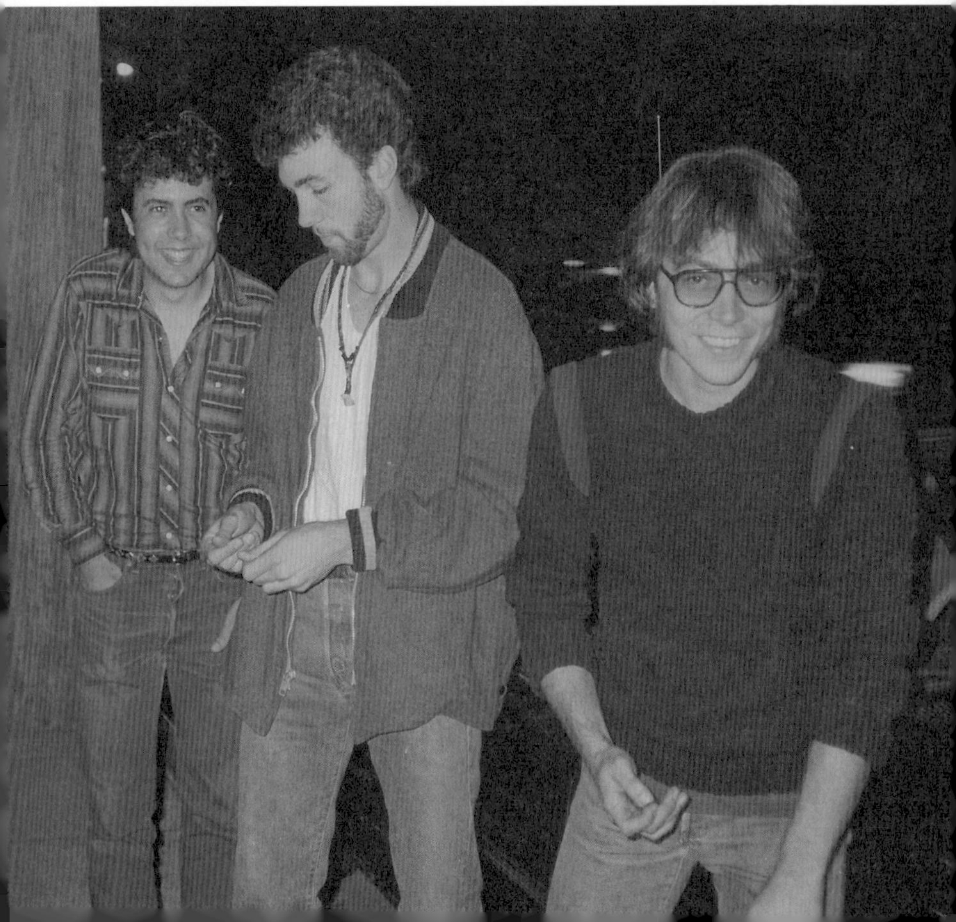

HOW IT STARTS

NO ONE FUCKS US, WE FUCK OURSELVES.

Karma, altruism, righteousness, call it what you will but it's hardwired into our mammalian brains. Abandonment is a separate matter entirely...

Bubba producing had upped the ante and Chez and Jackson rightly resented his bet.

Fuck this guy and his love of compression!

Squeezed out by a Loony Tune cartoon, it couldn't have been easy....

Bubba hated the drummer and things turned ugly with Chez and Jackson catching the brunt. Hell, I had no loyalty to the Mutant, he was the FNG, a walking derm abrasion who kept the chicks away. But Chez and Jackson were my brothers...

Dudens!

Damn it, embrace this guy. Learn something. It's time to reach out and expand. Jackson, gobble up "Green Onions" till you puke, Chez, play half as many notes half as often.

Didn't happen. The skies grew dark...

A sonic nervous breakdown.

Fuck!

SO LOW

ON SOME LEVEL I BLAMED THE BAND FOR LOSING ROBIN.

The truth is she left me when she figured I wouldn't drown clutching a five thousand dollar publishing check. All those dead babies sleeping between us didn't help. Then there was the kidney operation when her mom and sister demanded I screw 'em both on the same weekend.

No thanks, I barely fuck the patient anymore.

Something just gets sapped out of you playing rock n' roll. Sure, you're horny on the road (especially with a good drummer) but back home you just want to sit around, smoke weed and watch TV. It's like sex becomes a part of the gig, and if I ain't getting paid then why bother? You need an audience to cut one from the herd and brand that filly before the sun rises.

Sadly, more times than I'd like to admit, I awoke with a mouth full of kinky hair yet still suffering great balls of fire.

That would be alcohol's doing.

Is it too late for a refund?

Billy still cared enough to put Memphis together, thank god for that. Big Dog, oddly enough, quit when the band went on salary but Billy liked the idea of getting paid. Perhaps he envisioned a mighty gouge or maybe he figured he still had something to learn but we certainly arrived in rocking good shape and ready to solve that age old mystery:

Who the fuck shot Al Jackson?

Songs come in batches and this lot was a doozy. Bubba called for a pow-wow and I made it clear that the band was finished and this was my movie.

Sure, whatever you say Marlowe.

The next day we headed down to Sun to get some love from a land-locked narwhal who Bubba just adored.

So far so good.

Memphis is psychedelic enough without the acid.

I hazily recall sitting on the same toilet as Elvis, nice and warm too. Later, a Soviet wrestler dropped by with Sam's son but what really got me was the Afro Sheen goo on the headphones from a gospel session the night before.

Bubba just shrugged.

"Why you wearing those cans anyway? Just listen to the room."

Behind an ancient kit, Bubba started beating out a primal swagger.

Billy played a fucked up riff, barbed wire stretched too tight. I let out a yelp, my tail caught in the musical meat grinder.

"Get me back to Africa, I'm gonna be the black Howard Hughes!"

I had a real thing for Howard back then. Flying coast to coast, I believed the lit up electric grid from thirty thousand feet was his synapses and neurons still firing away. I dreamed of Mormon FBI agents bringing me all the codeine Buffy Sainte-Marie didn't want, and Brigham Young happily checking my piss bottles.

A man needs his obsessions.

Eventually, the Marcus Garvey by way of Don King revelatory stomp petered out and we headed to the control booth for a listen. The narwhal cocked his head.

"You boys ever think about going to Nashville and getting into *songwriting*?"

He was completely serious and no wonder. This studio had seen the craziest shit ever become the soundtrack of the world. I was deaf to his advice but Billy put that one away for later.

It would come in handy.

The Sunday School was next, a huge complex of state of the art recording facilities with a born again staff. It was a funny place where the sin or salvation see-saw went up and down to a modern beat. The evangelical air made it a safe place to go nuts, just like your average mega-church today. A lot of hits were being cut there at the time, while the past in the form of a one hit wonder or two would show up to service the Coke machine. I let my mutt run wild and got an earful from a certain soul singer who is more afraid of black dogs than hot grits let me tell you.

Billy and I really dug it.

Bubba had a more pained time. He was the red headed step-child of the Memphis scene and kept expecting that the Mr. Rodgers who ran the place would finally acknowledge his importance. Wasn't he bringing in money to the church? More importantly, wasn't he bringing in LA money? Boiling over, Bubba threatened to take his ball and go home but Billy just laughed while the engineer gave me a wink. I think a Tuinal saved the day, along with some vanilla yoghurt with shaved coconut sprinkled on top.

Bubba loved both.

The record itself was a breeze. The good ones are like that, effortless fun that just flows. All the bombastic wailing of the last record fell away to reveal a new smartass determination that was even a little sexy. We were playing like men, not boys and I was excited about flying solo with a killer wingman to boot. Fuck yeah, career move baby, take my rightful place with the real honchos like that Aussie preacher and Manchester's creepy poet.

Here's to you Robin...

You're gonna miss me...

There was just one problem.

I didn't have a record deal.

REVEREND LUTHER

YOU HEAR STORIES.

Like the day Elvis died and Bubba was driving an old pick-up back from Nashville. He had just had hemorrhoid surgery and there he was on I-40, listening to the radio, squirming up and down on one of those little inflatable doughnuts.

Crying like a baby...

We heard that one at a BBQ down in Hernando Mississippi. What a sweet wife. Bubba pouring ketchup on his steak. After jamming with the kids, Billy and I got lost trying to get back to Memphis.

Moonless night, darker than Mississippi mud.

We wind up at a crossroads for real and get out to try to find a sign or something.

Couple of rednecks in a farm truck drive by and just stare...

Scared the living fuck out of us.

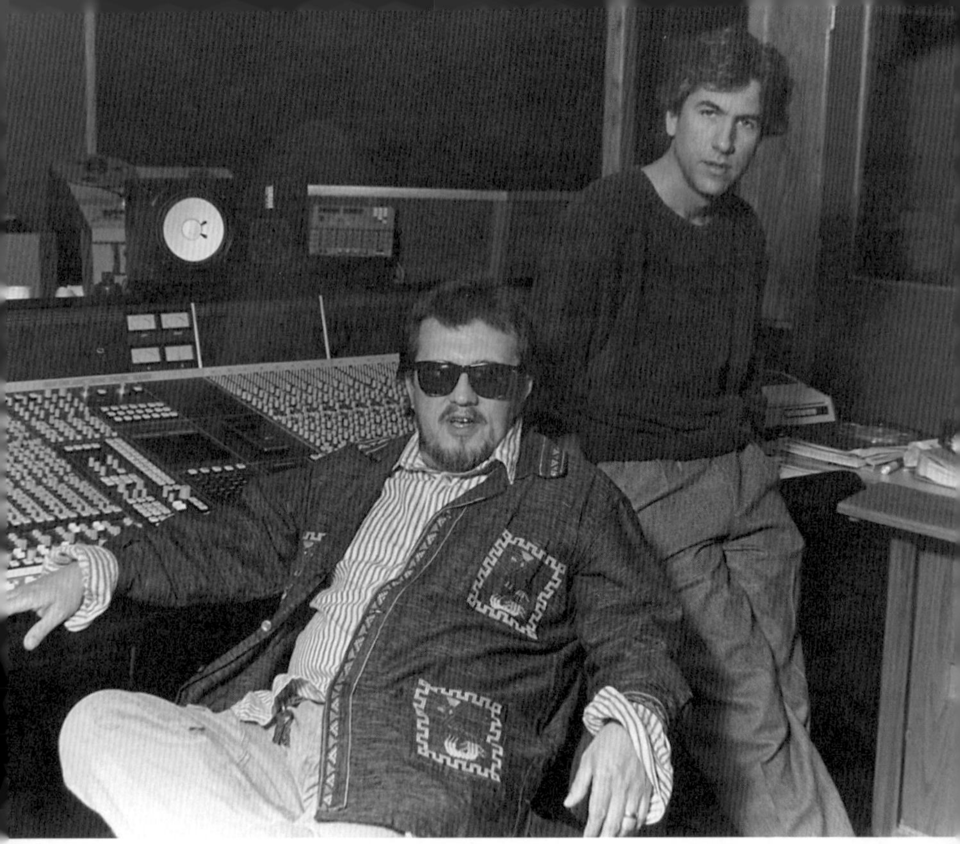

NEVER ANSWER THE PHONE

IT WAS A TRINITY.

I had found Billy and Billy had found Bubba.

Father, son and holy shit.

Mr. Rodgers knocked on the door. I had just nailed a vocal, pulled it right out of my ass.

"Marlowe, uh, sorry to disturb, Pink Elephant faxed over the contract. Your manager wanted you to be aware of Section 2, Clause 13."

"Yes?"

"It implies that both you and Billy are to be signed as the band, uh the name you previously have been performing under, it's not to be a solo record."

"No fucking way!"

At that the Sunday School principal allowed his sports jacket to swing open revealing a snub nose revolver in a shoulder holster. The riots were always just yesterday in Memphis, not to mention the War of Northern Aggression.

"Well there's the matter of your bill, Marlowe. Quite substantial at this point."

"Oh well."

Billy piped up...

"Shit it don't matter. Look at The Fall, or Jeffrey Lee..."

Bubba cleared his throat...

"It's your band Marlowe, everyone knows that."

Sure, everyone but Jackson and Chez, they would hear it from strangers.

They smile in your face...

Mr. Rodgers put the contract down on the mixing console and dramatically removed a pen from his pocket protector and placed it on top. He left me with this...

"You ever wonder Mr. Billings, just who shot Al Jackson?"

A NIGHT OFF

AFTER A TOUR OR TWO THE CREW BECOMES THE BAND and the band becomes a necessary evil. Since it's just Billy and me now, the other musicians are treated worse than groupies.

The crew rules all.

I love our South London pirates but they have some nasty friends who like the flick of a blade or the planting of a pint glass in some unlucky fellow's face. We *always* get paid and are never harassed at borders, even the dogs won't sniff. The lads instill fear in those that deserve it and for everyone else, well, they provide amusement and a bit of a laugh.

If you're lucky.

Edinburgh is a fucked up place. Too many unspeakable acts in the bowels of the castle, too many injustices never avenged. Glasgow has a certain gritty meanness to it but Edinburgh is a sweet looking lass who smiles for no one. Fuck her and fuck the Admiral's friends who are borderline psychotics with too much affection for National Front politicians and methamphetamine.

We are at a very expensive restaurant behaving badly and the citizens are scared shitless but I'm too bored to care. Billy's off with saner company, planning his future and making new friends who'll come in handy later.

Little brother is nobody's fool.

The punks start a food fight, they must have seen it in a movie.

Dinner's over.

Some shops are still open as we pour out. The lads disappear into a dive shop … football hooligan Wobbly loves to scuba when he's not rioting abroad. I head back to the hotel to sleep off the lamb chops and brandy, a bit randy from Wobbly's girlfriend squeezing my knee under the table. She wanted me to tickle her tasty bits but I was too much the coward what with Wobbly across the table giving me his sickish grin. Like most Americans, I would rather catch a bullet than get stabbed. Britain is one big facial scar, nothing polite about it at all.

I awake to screams of laughter and a weird *thwump*. The phone rings.

"Sir, I implore you to do something about members of your party in room 213. We don't wish to call the authorities but…"

Fuck!

I go to investigate, a couple of knocks and the Admiral opens up a crack, eyeball twitching.

"Yes Marlowe?"

"Dude, the desk is going to call Scotland Yard."

I wedge myself in and take a gander. No can't be, must be dreaming. Wobbly's girlfriend is trussed to the wall, hanging up off the ground like a spider gone splat. Wobbly's got a spear gun and is taking aim.

Thwump!

The spear impales itself into the wall about two inches from her head. She gives me a wink.

"Jesus Fucking Christ!"

"C'mon Yank give it a go…"

"Fuck no, give me that thing!"

This does not go over well at all. Even the target shakes her head. Wobbly starts frothing…

"How 'bout I shoot you with it, eh?"

I look at the Admiral who shrugs, it's the law of the sea and I'm on my own.

"Fuck you Wobbly, let's see if you have the balls she does…"

He gives me an odd look, laughs and pulls the spear from the wall. He reloads the gun and hands me the crossbow. Gracefully, he assumes the position next to his love.

"Fire away Yank."

The Admiral finds this all terribly amusing, he shouts out a wait and puts a stinky rolled up sock on top of Wobbly's head.

"Just like Robin Hood!"

Or Burroughs...

I aim way to the left but never mind, Wobbly panics and lurches in the same direction.

Thwump!

The spear tears through Wobbly's armpit nailing him to the wall. He screams like a little fucking baby...

"You've done it now Marlowe!"

The Admiral leaps into action and attends to his babbling mate. I sit on the bed and stare into space while Wobbly's girl lets out a nervous giggle. The Admiral turns around and gives me a smirk.

"Nice shooting that Marlowe, you pinned him to the wall using only his shirt, not a drop of blood."

Wobbly slides down to the carpet in relief. I toss him his toy and give his gal a pinch as I head for the door.

Burroughs said he owed it all to his wife's death.

I didn't owe anybody anything...

SIN EATER

I MEAN WHOSE ASS IS ON THE LINE HERE?

Musicians are so quick to denigrate this or celebrate that when the truth is we're all a bunch of cowards who rarely do anything without calculation. The business has imploded under the weight of mediocrity. Fuck I'm so tired of propping up bastards who don't know what's important, way more than any resentment towards me for failure to carry a tune.

Shit I can *do* things: argue a case, stop a bullet, discover shifting tectonics.

It is my duty as an *artiste* to seek the conceit of others who might fellate me into a calm state of normalcy. I don't ask for much, that's for sure, but please realize who is doing the work here that keeps you from connecting the exhaust pipe of my nightmares to the passenger window of your dreams.

A friend advised to let the meat rest before carving.

But for how long?

Until they know better?

The talented have nothing but.

I have less still.

It's enough.

PAPERS PLEASE

I ALWAYS HAD STRESS DREAMS where I couldn't remember lyrics or get equipment to work on stage. The worst scenario was when the bus takes off after a gig leaving me no money or passport and no one speaks English. That in itself is nonsensical since anyone with a high school education speaks some English, at least in Northern Europe. I'd awake very agitated and remind myself to keep my shit together, c'mon dude.

I was in a blackout I guess. We are on a ferry crossing the channel; the bus is dark and gently rocking, everyone asleep in their berths. I go out to explore. I am dressed in a white suit with a canary yellow pith helmet. I thought it would make me look *writerly*, but the hooligans on the stairs think I'm a poof and tell that to my face. I about face aft where the Tory bar is located. I need to watch my language up here in first class, that's a requirement. I would rather drink in the working class bar with the lads but fear for my life.

I should have gone with a safari suit instead...

Some old cow starts rubbing my leg at the bar. The English have the ugliest women in the world, all that butter and cheese and nasty meat pies. I find the head and smoke a little hash to keep me honest. When I return the cow has gone back to her stall leaving me her tab. Cheers! I find a booth and settle in. Tom is belting out "Delilah" and I think of mine. I see Robin's face as I nod off, drool pooling on my chest.

A jolt, my head snaps up.

I notice that the bar is empty and it is light outside. I can't detect any movement, we've arrived. Sweet fucking hell, there's a gig tonight, Berlin? Slowly, almost crawling, I head back down to the bus but the stairs are empty as is the car and truck level. Panicking, I make my way off the ferry with a few stragglers. I find myself in customs with no passport and just a few English pounds. The agents don't look amused and shrug when I speak American. Didn't we win the fucking war you miserable Krauts? I gesticulate and threaten and finally collapse in a chair and start to weep.

I feel a tap on my shoulder. It's the Admiral picking up a puppy at the pound.

"Off on a little adventure eh?"

Smiling, the Admiral had known where I was the entire time but wanted to teach me a lesson. I was dope sick and very much shaken from my fears being realized in such an overt manner. The whole tour seemed like a reckoning of sorts that I just wasn't prepared for, a coming to terms that I very much wanted to avoid. I wanted to be anywhere but in the here and now, the awful present.

Dreaming is for losers who just can't make it work...

THE JUNKY'S DILEMMA

THE TRAIN STATION IN COPENHAGEN WAS ALWAYS A FAVORITE.

The streets radiating away from the depot were prime scoring spots. International copping time is around 4pm, although there's usually an early morning trade if you know where to look. Night is when the knives and bunk comes out. In Denmark, the dope was always the same: snow white and her seven whores. We'd hole up in a cheap hotel and have a good nod. "Paris Texas" was always the in-house movie.

Harry Dean never got the girl.

The rhythm section hated it when Billy and I were fucked up, there was nothing to hold back. Guitars are usually fighting to get away, a crashing shore break. Musically, I loved squatting down in that big fat pocket and scratching my balls. I'd get so far behind the beat I felt like a satellite in an elliptical orbit, edging farther and farther away from radio contact. Unfortunately, we weren't playing jazz, or even the blues.

Rock n' roll is a loaded spring, *it's the potential that matters.*

Jagger once said that if you were a sculptor or something then being a junky might be a pretty good lifestyle. The problem is the world doesn't reduce things down to their basic elements like dope does.

Nothing does.

THE CAPPUCCINO

THERE IS SOMETHING JUST A BIT OFF...

I walk in and for a second I thought I had entered the wrong room. I hear a faucet dripping and take a look in the bathroom. There Abby floats in the avocado tub with candles burning and empty pill jars galore. She looks beautiful, like Cindy Sherman posing as Lola Falana.

"What the fuck are you doing?"

I found out later that the front desk had simply let her up and a sympathetic maid had unlocked the door. That's the problem with becoming so familiar with one hotel, they treat you like family.

"Go die somewhere else you cunt!"

I pull her out and dry her off. No cut wrists, relief. She is mumbling absurdities and vows of love. I figure if she can stand she can breathe. I grab a pill bottle and take a look. Librium, more relief. There's no booze on her breath either... my lucky day.

"Get dressed Abby..."

She droops her head and lets out a wail.

"Shut up, this is England!"

I scoop up her clothes and push her to the door. I tell her I think she'll live and if I call the paramedics they'll lock her up in the psych ward....

"You wouldn't want that now, would you?"

She takes a wobbly swing that just misses. I push her out into the empty hallway and throw her clothes after her. She manages a very lucid goodbye.

"My father's gonna kill you..."

Him being Sicilian, I know she's not kidding. I hold my breath but she starts to scream and bang on the door. I calmly walk over to the phone.

"Yes, this is Mr. Billings in room 213, there is some crazed girl out in the hall, please remove her from the premises."

Billy and I saw Abby a couple months later. She was walking down Queensway with some friends. We were feasting on duck noodle soup while life passed by the large plate glass window. Billy had fucked her first so there was history all around. I was happy to see her laughing, joking with her pals. Passing the window, she turned to catch her image and saw us sitting there slurping our noodles.

The color drains from her beautiful mocha face.

Her friends catch her as she faints and help her towards the tube. Looking around, they are clueless as to the cause.

There's no band-aid for this, I'm horrified, still I wonder...

Billy, you ever fuck her in the ass?

THIS TIME AROUND

FIVE LONG YEARS LATER I WAS BACK IN HOLLYWOOD but I barely recognized it. Crack had come to town and AIDS had done its thing and it just wasn't fun anymore. Of course I'd gone to shit as well so we made a perfect couple. Billy and I were spending thousands of dollars a day with a producer we hated, cutting songs not worthy of being born. I tried to gather myself by seeing Robin but the conversations were strained and we both felt too damn old for our years. Driving down La Brea towards LAX and my waiting flight, Robin started weeping uncontrollably. I remembered that up here by the oil rigs was the way to the abortion clinic that we had visited an obscene amount of times.

I never went in, preferring to wait in the parking lot smoking a joint or two.

Misty morning blue there's nothing left to say...

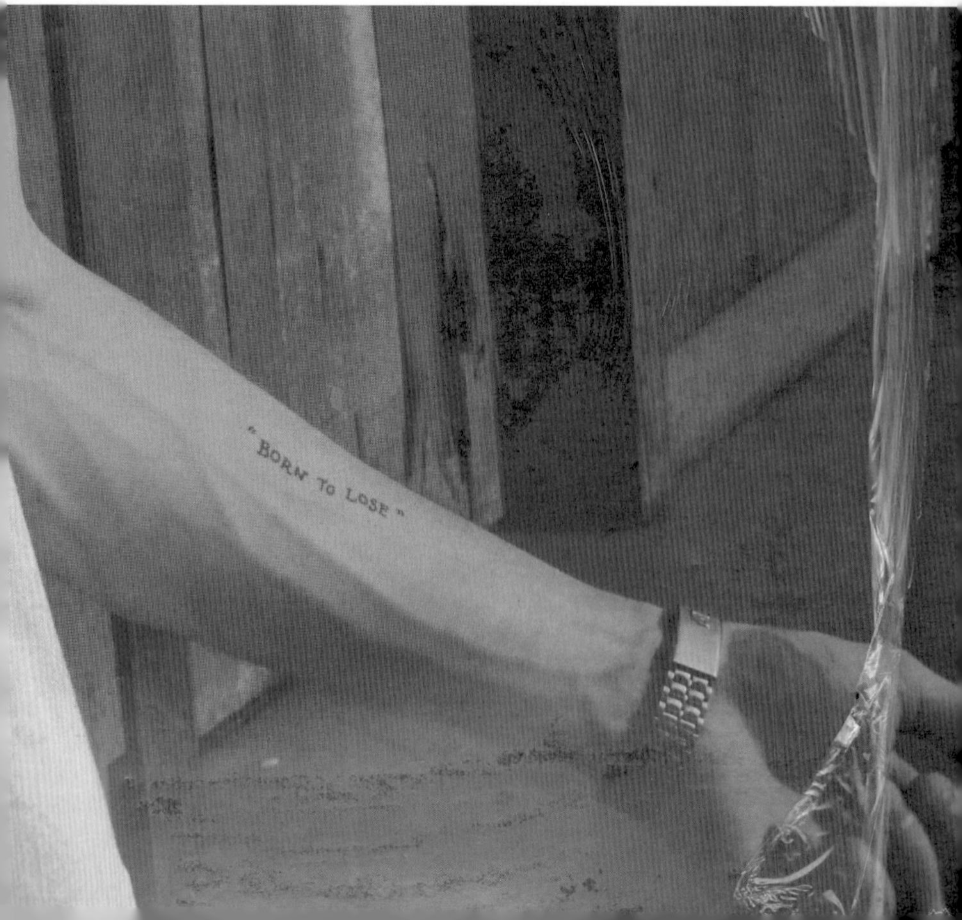
"BORN TO LOSE"

ALMOST BLUE

DOPE SICK, I NEED TO COP.

The Turks run the rackets and I have found *the man*. As a daughter brings me tea, he asks to buy my passport. He explains that I found no dope at the train station because a junky stabbed one of his dealers and he is punishing the entire class. He will sell me what I want but neglects to tell me that it is poison.

He hates me and I return his smile.

I wake Billy and show him my haul. He is neither happy nor surprised. We crane our necks to watch "The Rose" on the wall mounted TV. We know we are in Germany because it's dubbed without subtitles. The band is great, isn't that Steve Hunter? The maid has placed two bent spoons side by side on the dresser.

Sweet of her.

Morning now. We are lobsters on the autobahn driving to perdition. I am not religious but I feel the burn. Shit needs to happen and this is killing it, a cork stuck in the bottle. Our skin is mottled red from the tainted dope and Billy pukes out the window every couple of miles.

We are obliviously adrift, wary of rescue.

Someone wonders whether Chet jumped or was pushed from that window in Amsterdam.

Both?

SIZE FORTY LONG

WE ARE DECAYING FAST BUT STILL RADIOACTIVE.

Bands are like plutonium, they have lives and half-lives. There is plenty of pain control and still enough faith from the record company to keep us in per diems but little else. At a festival near Stonehenge, I find myself following Mr. New York himself to the public shithouse. I have no choice, but he has forsaken his private commode for the stench of community. I wanted to talk to him earlier (we both love the *roman noir*) but I shied away. He is quite the prick, everybody knows that. Walking behind him now, his ass looks like a bulldozer plowed through it. After several minutes, he leaves the plastic shitter and I enter to take my leak. Steaming on top of a mound of toilet paper is the legend's latest masterpiece. It occurs to me that I could probably sell it for several thousand dollars to one of his adoring fans.

Or better yet, cast it in bronze...

These encounters with history both personal and tertiary happen all tour long. It's like the Gods have come down from their penthouses to rub it in our faces. They seldom disappoint. In Scandinavia, the Canadian drifter shows up with Memphis' finest and comments on the breeze.

We are there as insurance in case someone cancels but understudies at our age? Sure enough, *someone's kid dies* and we take the stage.

So happy to be here everybody!

I notice a tough blonde chick checking us out from the wings. She sneers and reports back to her English mates who have never sold out to anybody anywhere. Their leader lives in Chicago now and supposedly has a dick bigger than Dillinger and a fat mamacita to put it into...

I'm jealous all around.

After our set, the blind genius plays. We ask the drummer how he got the gig?

"Same size suit..."

Of course...

Great stories to tell the grandkids, but really little else.

It was better with the Dudens, playing shitty little bars and having a ball.

The love is gone and it sure ain't the business' fault. That much was fine. Money is a very good reason for most everything. Don't let anyone tell you different, they're lying.

So what's left? For me, nothing much, find some sanity maybe. Billy still has a shot at something if he can survive the present. He made me promise a long time ago that I would never allow him to be buried with his guitar.

That's probably what saved him...

You have to understand the lie before you can embrace the truth.

TELL ME ABOUT THE FLOWERS

A DOCTOR'S OFFICE IN ROME... I'm drooling, acting like a retard.

Billy tells the croaker that he's in charge of me but that I can't sleep and it's keeping him up. I can't tell if the doc speaks English or not, he eyes us warily but could really give a shit. He shrugs and writes a scrip and I shuffle out holding Billy's hand.

A new low.

We walk into the first pharmacy we see and Billy hands the paper over. They've just had a delivery and I blurt out some nonsense while Billy pockets several packages of Xanax. It will mix nicely with the phenobarbital.

Lower still.

The cheap hotel has tiny bathtubs shaped like chairs. I sit and watch the water rise quite satisfied with the immediate present.

But the past and the future?

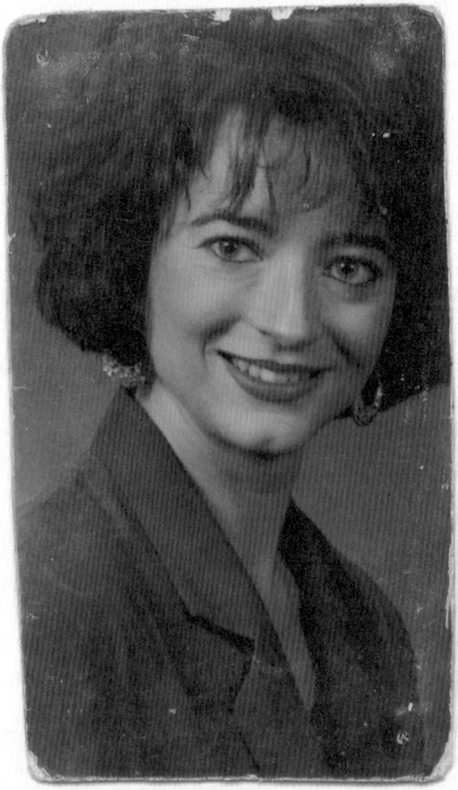

LOVE WILL KILL YOU

IT'S A BIG FESTIVAL, WE PLAY OKAY, WHATEVER.

Later the shutterbugs get their chance. I won't take off my shades... what a rock star.

There in the back I see something... *interesting.*

"Hey you slobs, let that belly button up front."

She puts the camera down and smiles. She's beautiful.

Her name is Maria but she goes by Lulu.

Too bad, I really needed a *Maria.*

I keep her prisoner in my hotel. Drawing a bath, I shoot up in the bathroom.

She has no idea.

Somewhere in London a man weeps all night.

I will be that man one day.

I'm that man now.

FINAL LAP

THAT LAST TOUR STARTED IN PHOENIX...

Phoenix?

Lanky got me started me with a little pill on the flight over and I proceded to cop my way through Europe easy as pie.

Bingo, bango, bongo...

It ended in Athens...

Athens... Greece?

I tried to cop from a junky with *a syringe tattooed on the palm of his hand.*

He didn't want to burn me, he actually took the time to make up a fake little bindle.

Junkies are funny that way.

Back at the hotel, looking up at my beautiful Lulu, then down at that very expensive corn starch, I knew which one I'd choose…

Now if the dope hadn't been bunk…

But it was.

And I stopped…

Everything.

Ain't no pictures in my book, the dirty pages take a look…

LA VIDA MUERTE

LONDON HAD NOT GONE WELL.

We fly in to Madrid and find a random hotel. It's on Gran Via across from Plaza España.

It could have been anywhere.

Lulu goes off in the morning to a job interview and I open the curtains.

Damn, look at those Africans hanging out. I bet they got some smoke.

I wander down and make some inquiries. A tall skinny negro opens his mouth and shows me the bindles of heroin.

Oh fuck.

I buy one out of nostalgia. Because of the police, he wants me to stash it in my mouth.

Are you crazy?

I go back to the hotel and snort the brown dope courtesy of the CIA in Afghanistan.

Sweet Home Alabama...

Lulu comes back all excited, she got the job! She looks me in the eye and her smile disappears.

Some things never change...

RUB & TUG

FROM REHAB TO JAPAN IN ABOUT A WEEK.

I take advantage of the layover in Paris to buy some codeine; each terminal has a pharmacy and I hit them all.

Loaded for bear.

In Tokyo, the first thing we do is get very drunk. The record company assigns us a very cute handler but Billy and I send her home to her boyfriend. We fear for her soul and virgin ass...

We wind up at the penthouse restaurant at the New Otani.

I wouldn't get out of bed for less than 300K a year...

So claims a Miami businessman who is shocked when we admit how little money we make.

Billy goes back to his room and the American takes me to Soapland. The middle aged whore scrubs and scrubs but is never satisfied.

The dirt just won't come off.

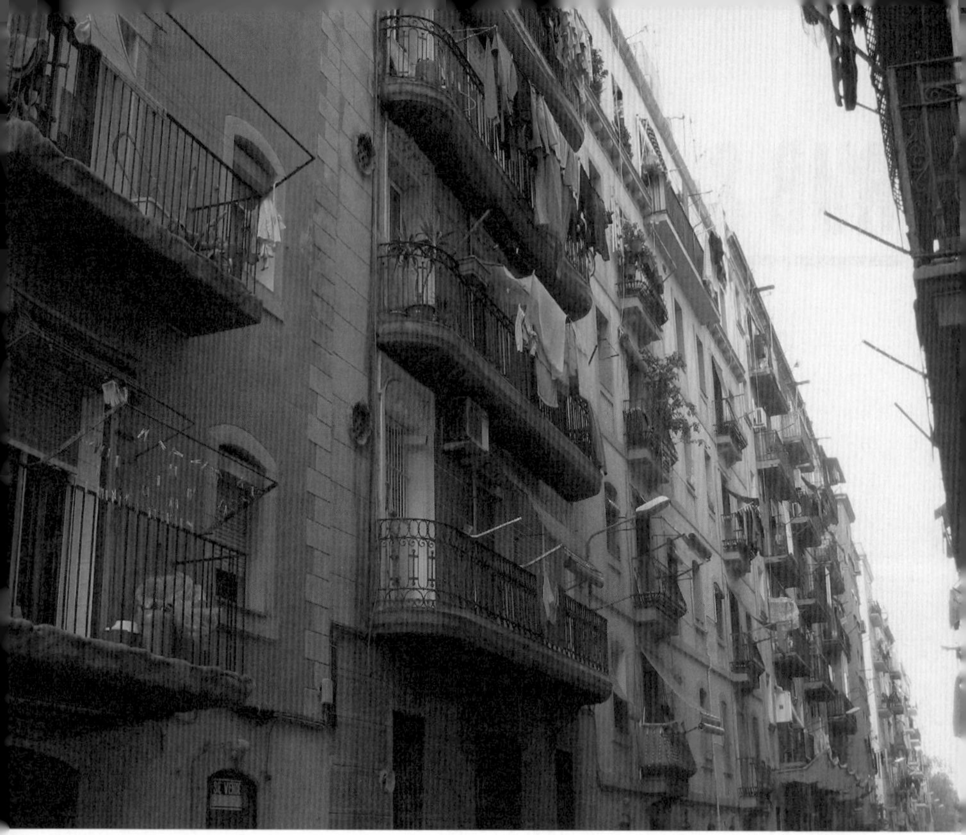

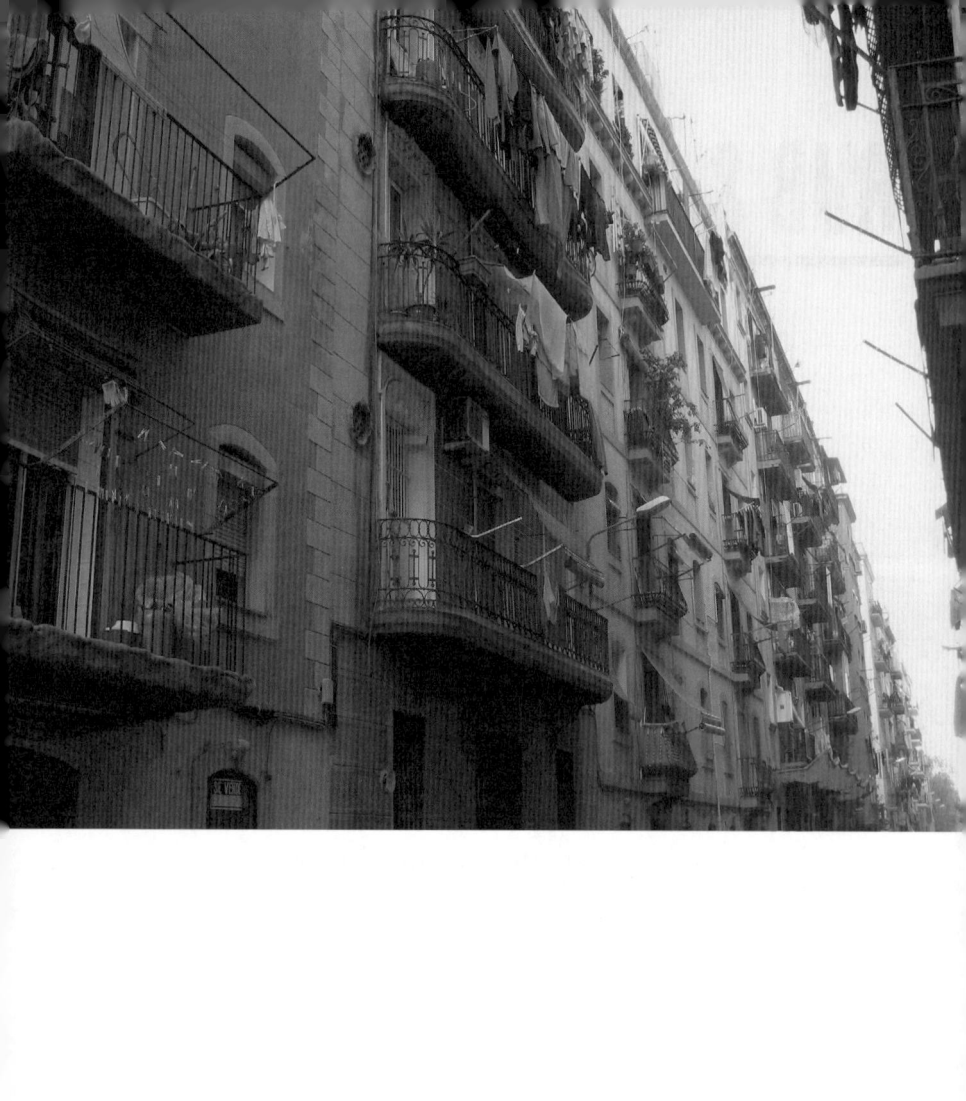

WAITING AT THE ALTAR

I START FEELING DOPE SICK AT THE CHURCH.

She's late, the brother has forgotten the rings, the priest is pissed.

It could have been so beautiful. Lulu walking the streets of the barrio in a dress made by her mother's hands. People clapping and crying all at once.

Lulu won't stop shaking. She never says "I do" but the priest doesn't care.

I start drinking at the reception… spanish brandy.

The bride and groom are expected to stay till the end, attending to the guests.

My Dad forgets his jacket. I accuse someone of stealing it.

I am beyond drunk, dope sick, crazy.

I call my bride a devil. She goes home in tears.

I spend the night alone...

Marriage over before it starts.

Crying, I tell all this to Billy in Germany a couple months later. The dope brings the curtain down. Tragedy in one act. I get a weird feeling and call his room.

No answer.

I convince the desk to give me a key and I find Billy twisted under himself, nodded out. Ken all over again. I slap him and walk him around the room, then around the block for an hour or two. The sun comes up painting our faces gold, we laugh and go back to our rooms.

Thanks man...

I take a bath and wake up freezing...

Little brother cannot absolve me.

God?

Don't make me laugh...

FROZEN IN MY HEADLIGHTS

WE MADE THAT LAST RECORD in Tucson at a drive-in studio.

I sing behind the wheel of a 69 Montego, holding on for dear life.

The songs are fine but the moment has passed and my heart is damaged beyond repair.

In the alley behind the studio, there's a dumpster with a shrine to the young beautiful creature whose dismembered parts had been discarded there a few months before. I go out and talk to her, asking if she forgives the monster who had cut her up. Cops drive by and pause to check me out, maybe it's him?

Ignoring them, I light a candle...

Guilty still.

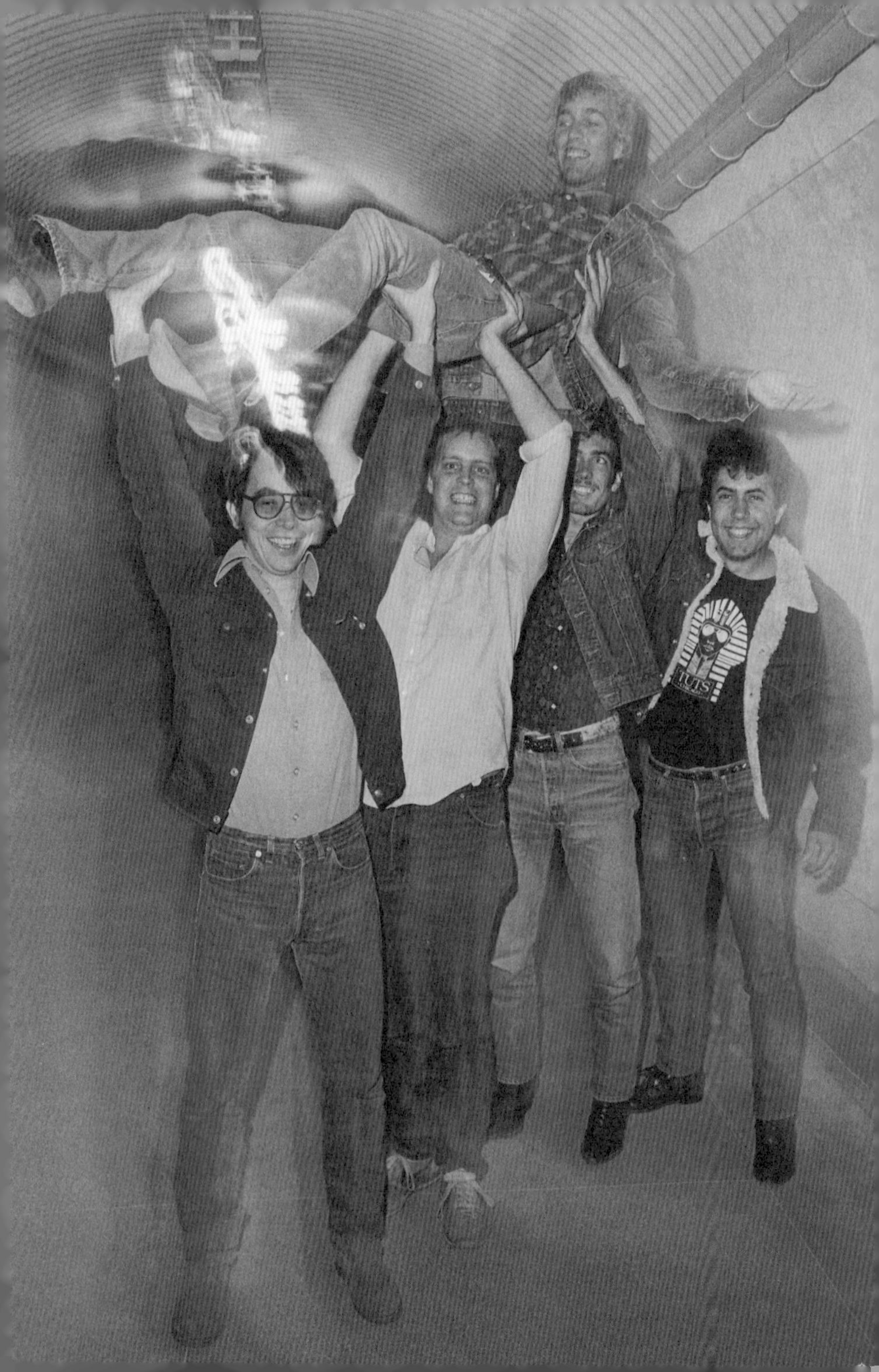
TUTS

ANY GOOD?

THE RESENTMENT WAS ALWAYS THERE....

Couldn't play, couldn't sing, the writing they left alone.

Maybe it was the reverberations of the original band, so pure and righteous and aloof.

My brothers... dudens.

But no, not really...

I benefited from an intellectual laziness that cajoled and fondled without thought or merit, sickening really. Don't get me wrong, I had my talents but that doesn't mean you provide critical and monetary support to that which should stay underground forever, if not jailed in some dank dungeon of despair.

Pop music should be popular, just like public space should be public. Now it's all just a means to an end, the path to the next debit purchase. We punks paid our dues up front, continually stepped on, now forever worthless.

We lost.

I always thought it would end the next day and one day it did. You can impose yourself on the world forever like a baboon showing his ass but don't expect people to keep on clapping. I'd had enough shame going back to my cowboy brother catching me with the family Hoover. To his credit he never brought it up again, but my face is still redder than my cock vibrating in that paper towel tube.

Getting away with bad art is devastating... soul killing.

Too much fun, not enough time, the party's over and I'm feeling fine...

THE RUBBER ROOM

I DON'T KNOW WHAT IT ALL MEANS, nothing much I suspect.

I did what I did and suffer for most of it and get mailbox money for the rest.

Robin finally had a baby...

Lulu ran off with a gypsy...

No one returns my calls.

Still, like a secret spring hidden back in the woods, the music keeps seeping through.

A brother-in-law tells me about some movie that got the credits wrong...

Peeling potatoes I hear a snippet on the radio between newscasts...

On the net there's an old interview that makes me cringe...

Someone shoot that guy.

Barely a footnote really.

I finally made it to the nut house. The staff was undecided about what to do. My last interview was with a psychiatric nurse: a fashionably dressed black man who loved Miles Davis.

"You used to play music? Made records did you?"

"More or less."

"If I was you, I would try to figure out why you did that, what made you *need* to do that."

So here we are.

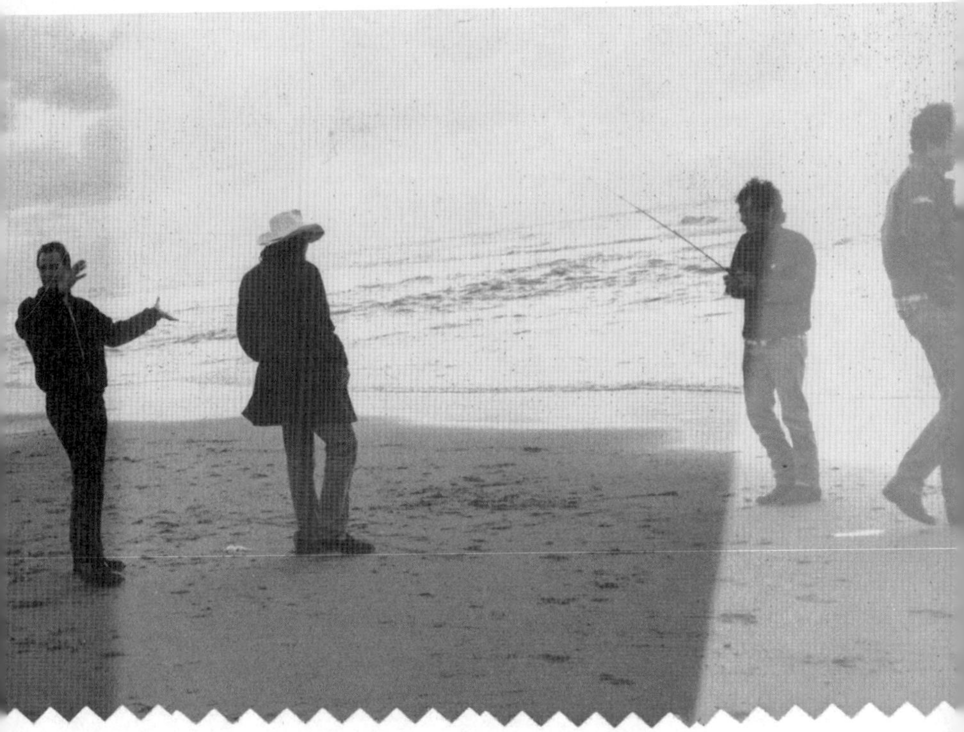

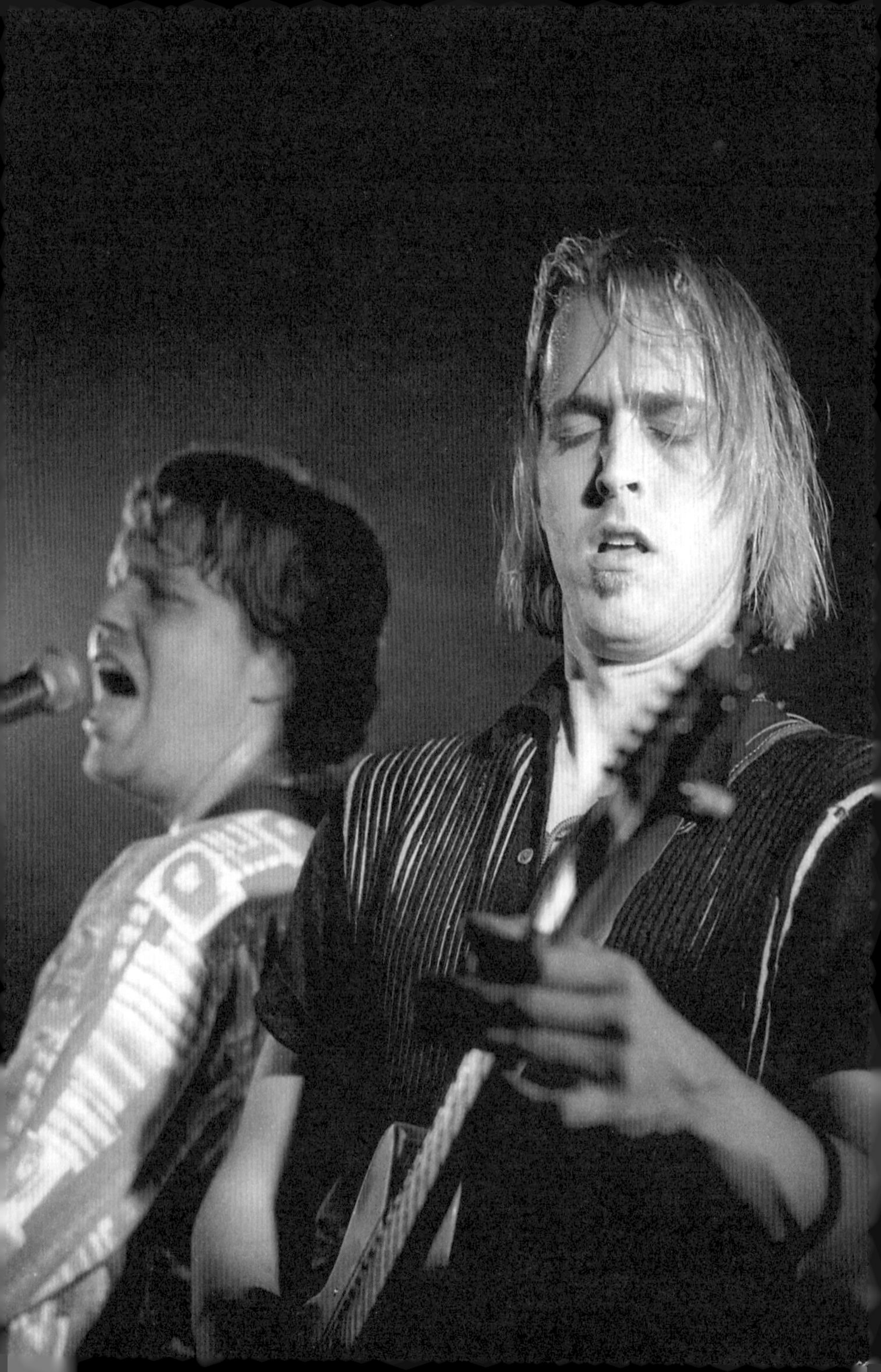

ACKNOWLEDGMENTS

THIS BOOK BEGAN AS AN EXCHANGE between myself and the late Guy Neal Williams. An editor at Serpent's Tail, John Williams, convinced me to keep it lean and mean and without any commercial potential. Javier Rosas Herrera's design softened the blow and allowed the text to transcend my petty motivations. The photographer Cliff GREEN endured my ever changing whims and delusions. Finally, Richard England at Cadiz Music agreed to expand a pathetic little pamphlet into something more substantial. I'm indebted to you all and thank everyone else who lifted a finger on my behalf. You know who you are...

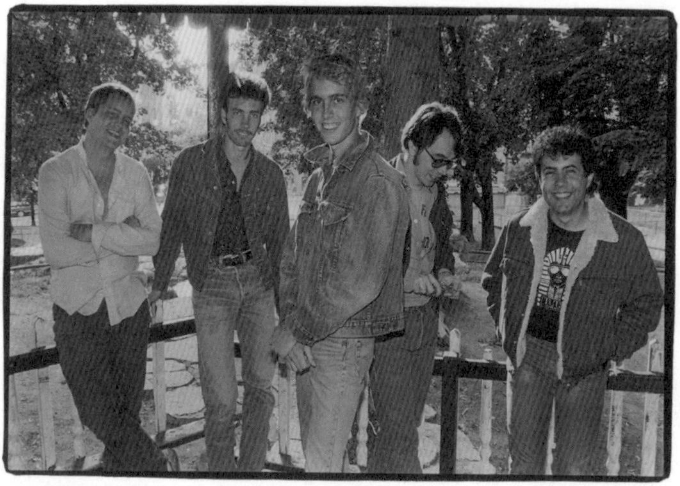

CREDITS

PHOTO CREDITS

Cliff GREEN: cover shot as well as pages 10, 28, 32, 39, 40, 48, 54, 92
Darren Andrews: pages 8, 146
Agustín García: page 14
Toby Dickens: page 47
Amy Mehaffey: page 53
Chris Metzler: page 74
Gilbert Blecken: page 114
Tana Coman: page 122 (album cover photo)
Dan Stuart: page 136

ALL OTHER IMAGES PHOTOGRAPHER(S) UNKNOWN.

CONTACT INFO

Cadiz Music: cadizmusic.co.uk
Dan Stuart: marlowebillings.com
Javier Rosas Herrera: javierrosasherrera.com
Cliff GREEN: cliffs-photos.com
Darren Andrews: darrenandrewsphotos.co.uk
Toby Dickens: escapeintolife.com/photography/toby-dickens
Amy Mehaffey: facebook.com/cookwoman23
Chris Metzler: decorrecords.com
Gilbert Blecken: gilbertblecken.wordpress.com
Tana Coman: tanacoman.com

THE DELIVERANCE OF MARLOWE BILLINGS
by Dan Stuart was printed and bound
by Productos Gráficos El Castor in
Oaxaca, México.
The typesetting and page design was
done using Adobe InDesign.
The headlines are set in the font
League Gothic and the text is set in
Minion, 10.5 point on a 13 point line.

*This edition is limited to
1,000 copies.*